DISASTER DOWN THE LINE

DISASTER DOWN THE LINE

Train Accidents of the 20th Century

J.A.B. Hamilton

JAVELIN BOOKS

POOLE·NEW YORK·SYDNEY

First published in 1967 by George Allen & Unwin as
'British Railway Accidents of the Twentieth
Century'

This edition published 1987 by Javelin Books, Link
House, West Street, Poole, Dorset BH15 1LL

Distributed in Australia by
Capricorn Link (Australia) Pty Ltd
PO Box 665, Lane Cove
NSW 2066

ISBN 0 7137 1973 7

Printed and bound in Great Britain by
The Guernsey Press Co., Guernsey, C.I.

CONTENTS

Foreword

FOREWORD

Exactly sixty years have passed since Alfred Rosling Bennett brought out his work on *Moving Accidents by Steam and Rail* describing some of the disasters which had shocked the Victorians. No comparable work has yet appeared dealing with the great accidents of the present century. The literature on the subject is meagre indeed. H. Raynar Wilson's book on accident statistics, published in 1925, provides a useful analysis of all railway accidents up to that date, but contains no descriptive matter. J. Thomas's *Obstruction—Danger* published in 1937 gives slightly sensationalized accounts of numerous accidents at home and abroad, including a few of those recorded here. In a different category is L. T. C. Rolt's work *Red for Danger,* which gives a comprehensive review of accidents in their relation to the development of safety measures, and is likely to remain the standard work on that aspect of the subject. My purpose has been to do for the twentieth century what Bennett did for the nineteenth : to put on record the story of some of the most notable British railway disasters of our time, with the help primarily of official reports and the contemporary press.

I have chosen twenty-seven great accidents since 1900, and they are set out in chronological order. Any selection of this kind is bound to provoke controversy, and I can only plead that I have tried to make the choice on as logical a basis as possible. Every accident finds a place in which the death-roll has exceeded twenty. The number killed is of course no necessary yardstick of the seriousness of an accident, still less of its interest. In some of the most destructive accidents recorded here the death-roll was relatively small, simply because the train concerned was not carrying many passengers. I have therefore included disasters with a lower casualty list which seemed to justify a place by reason of their spectacular character or other special interest, with the proviso that the number of killed amounted to at least ten.

A word of explanation may be in place here. In all accidents the harrowing details are extensively reported in the press. That is natural, for calamity makes news. But such descriptions, dramatic enough in a single case, would in a book of accidents become intolerably repetitious. Only in the case of the super-catastrophe at Quintinshill have I allowed myself a little latitude in this respect.

These chronicles then are in some sense a record of the second half of the age of steam. By 1900 railway operation had shed its earlier crudities. Continuous brakes on passenger trains had been compulsory for eleven years; refinements of block working, like the Sykes lock-and-block system or the Tyer electric tablet system on single lines, were in use in many places. But all-wooden coaches were still numerous and gas-lit ones in the great majority. Safeguards against a signalman's failures were far from complete, and there were no safeguards at all against a driver's failure to observe the signals. Railwaymen were still grossly overworked (and poorly paid); in the case of some of the earlier accidents we may at least suspect that fatigue played a contributory part.

By the time of our last accident in 1962 we have reached the fully-modernized railway system. All-wooden coaches have given place to the steel-framed sort and these again to all-steel ones; buck-eye couplings and Pullman vestibules have greatly reduced the danger of telescoping. Gas-lit coaching stock is an ancient memory. In the realm of signalling the track circuit, in its infancy in 1900, is now universal on all main lines. Colour-light signals, then unthought-of, are increasingly becoming the rule. Automatic warning to drivers by audible cab signals, bravely pioneered by the Great Western Railway as long ago as 1906, is at long last being applied to main lines generally, though its application is still far from complete.

Beyond all this is the revolution in motive power. However much we may grieve at the passing of steam—and I for one am an unashamed mourner at its grave—we must agree that the new forms of power are immensely more efficient and safer. The ease of handling, the flexibility, the mere better visibility, of diesel and electric traction in themselves hold the promise of a more accident-free future.

So we may come to look back on the Quintinshills, the Harrows and the rest as nightmares of a vanished era. If that is so, it is appropriate that a book of accidents should appear now, as the railways emerge into the new age. New hazards of course may arise. Already we have learned of the threat of fire in diesel multiple units, while the ugly menace of children's sabotage has reared its head in some industrial areas. Doubtless all such dangers will be countered in due course. There remains the eternally fallible human element, which no safeguards can wholly eliminate.

It is usual in a book like this to quote a bibliography, but beyond the works I have mentioned there is really no bibliography to quote. I have however a number of acknowledgements to make. First of all I would thank the Ministry of Transport for putting its records and reports at my disposal; without these it would have been impossible even to consider writing this book. I would also record my grateful thanks to Mr Rolt for allowing me to use portions of his material; I would mention particularly his description of track circuiting, which I have followed closely in Chapter 6. My thanks too are due to Mr Hamilton Ellis and his publishers for permission to use material from his book *The Trains We Loved*, which will be found in the chapter on Salisbury, and to Mr J. G. Holmes for permission to draw on his carefully-researched article on Quintinshill which appeared in the *Railway World*. I would add a special word of thanks to a group of Charfield informants, notably Police Constable Donald Gibbard, who has made himself an authority on that accident, Mr Harry Smith and Mr Fred Ayres. My thanks go lastly to various railway officials, among whom I might mention the stationmasters at Castlecary and Ditton Junction, who were good enough to give me their time and whose ready help made the writing of this book possible.

J. A. B. Hamilton

CHAPTER 1

HALL ROAD

LANCASHIRE & YORKSHIRE RAILWAY

Our first accident, strangely enough, concerns two electric trains. It happened at Hall Road, about seven miles from Liverpool on the Lancashire & Yorkshire Railway's Southport line, on the evening of July 27, 1905.

At this early date progressive Merseyside already had three electric railways. The Liverpool Overhead Railway, the world's first overhead electric line, came first in 1893. Ten years later Liverpool scored another first, for the Mersey Railway was the earliest in Britain to convert from steam to electric working. The electrification of the Southport line in the following year, 1904, represented yet another pioneer achievement, for it was the first conversion by a main-line railway.

The early years of the century were unlucky ones for Liverpool's railways, for they suffered a succession of accidents. In the tunnel at Dingle, on the Liverpool Overhead Railway, two days before Christmas 1901, six persons had died in a fire caused by a fusing of one of the train motors. Eighteen months later, at Waterloo, two stations from Hall Road on the same Southport line while still in its steam-worked days, an excursion train had been derailed and seven passengers killed. Hall Road made an unhappy third.

The Southport line was very nearly not built at all. Indeed we may say that it owed its existence to the pertinacity of an unknown Southport gentleman. Having obtained powers to build the line, the Company took fright. Once past the Liverpool suburbs the country was in those days comparatively empty, and it was feared that the line would not pay. So construction hung fire until the said gentleman, irked by the delay, obtained a High Court order of Mandamus compelling the Company to go ahead. Thus pushed into it the Lancashire & Yorkshire discovered that it had a gold mine. A lively suburban traffic quickly built up, and the commuter ('contract ticket holder' was then the phrase) began to make his appearance. It was a commuter train which came to grief at Hall Road.

At that time there was a 10-minute service from Liverpool Exchange to Hall Road, where alternate trains terminated, as a few rush-hour ones still do today. These were run forward into a centre siding, there to wait until reversing out on to the up platform ready for the return journey. There were also a few peak-hour fasts, and it was one of these that was involved: the 6.30 from Exchange, first stop Formby, two stations beyond Hall Road. Those were the days for commuters! A train with a seating capacity of 350 contained 67 passengers, 20 of them first-class.

The previous train, the 6.20, finished at Hall Road. Having discharged its passengers it was run forward on to the centre siding, and Signalman Boote re-set the points for the express. The siding points were protected by the inner home signal, and an electrical detector prevented this being lowered unless the switch-blades of the points were absolutely in their true position. As the points were connected with the signal box by 200 yards of rodding this required a strong pull by the signalman, and there had been cases of the signal failing to 'come off'. The last occasion had been about two months before.

The same thing happened again now. Boote pulled off his outer home signal, close to the box, and the starter, but the inner home refused to move, and so also, naturally, did the inner and outer distants. As the express approached, slowed by both distants at caution, Boote replaced his outer home and starter while he tried to get the inner home to work. He pulled the levers three times vigorously, but unfortunately at the end of the operation left them set for the siding.

By this time Boote was getting anxious. The express was coming up to his box and was very nearly at a standstill, and he had heard of signalmen being fined for stopping a fast train unnecessarily. If he had looked down his frame he would have seen that the points lever was reversed. But he did not think to do so, and of course the signal still would not move.

There is a drill prescribed for such situations. Here is the extract from the rule book, slightly shortened:

'When a signal becomes defective, or is not working efficiently, a competent person must be placed at such signal with hand signal and detonators, and act under the instructions of the signalman.'

If this had been done, the position of the points would immediately have been noticed. But it would have taken time. It would have meant fetching the stationmaster and his finding someone to send to the signal, and here was the express being held up. Boote, in his apprehension, took the short way out. Concluding that the detector mechanism was out of order he again pulled off his outer home and starter, and waved a green flag to the motorman as a sign that the latter could pass the inner home.

The motorman, Rimmer, had no business to obey the flag signal. He knew the rule as well as Boote, but he claimed afterwards that he saw the inner home at clear, which was impossible. It is the first of several instances we shall encounter where someone thought he saw something different to what was there. A study of railway accidents is an education in the human power of self-deception.

Thus given the clear, Rimmer, who had nearly stopped, put on full power. Never was the accelerative power of electricity more dramatically demonstrated. In 350 yards or so the express had worked up to over 40 m.p.h. when it hit the standing train in the siding. Rimmer might have checked speed when he found himself being carried into the siding, but apparently he was too surprised to do so. He was badly injured in the crash.

The local was standing with its brakes partly on. The express pushed it forward, its wheels skidding, for 50 yards. According to an observer, the rear coach of the local was shot into the air and descended on to the front coach of the express; both its bogies were pushed under the second coach, which was thus supported by four bogies. The damage was extraordinarily localized. Apart from the two coaches actually involved not a pane of glass was broken in either train. But twenty-one passengers were killed or died of injuries, and most of the remainder were either injured or had to be treated for shock. Most of those killed were said to have had their heads crushed in.

Ten of the dead were women, mostly unmarried and in their twenties—doubtless the advance guard of that army of secretaries which was still something of a novelty in city offices.

Though Merseyside, as I have said, had known electric traction for a matter of years, the accident caused some local alarm, and at the inquest the Coroner found it desirable to utter reassuring words. He trusted the travelling public would not be disposed to think that the electric service between Southport and Liverpool was not safe. So far as he could make out, the calamity had nothing to do with the electrification of the railway.

The jury found both Boote and Rimmer censurable, but not criminally so. In its wisdom it added that facing points should be abolished wherever feasible.

The question of facing points also worried the *Liverpool Echo*, which took it upon itself to castigate the Company:

'Had there been no facing points the calamity would not have occurred. The blame therefore must rest on the Lancashire & Yorkshire Railway Company for adopting at this particular station an arrangement sanctioned by expert theory and practice at terminal stations only'

—disregarding the fact that Hall Road was a terminal station in respect of half its trains.

The *Railway Magazine* had a different criticism. It pontificated in a manner which would bring blushes to its sophisticated descendent today:

'One of the advantages claimed for electric traction is high acceleration, and if the speed this unfortunate train had attained in so short a distance be due to "high acceleration" then "high acceleration" is far from an unmixed blessing'.[1]

In fact electric traction in this country has had a very good accident record. Much later in this book we shall encounter other cases in which electric trains were involved, but in only one was an electric train the actual destructive agent, and then it was a signalman's fault. For a long time yet we shall be concerned only with steam trains.

[1] *Railway Magazine*, September 1905.

CHAPTER 2

SALISBURY

LONDON & SOUTH WESTERN RAILWAY

Twice within a few months in 1906 a train sped through a station at night to destruction on the curve beyond. It happened first at Salisbury, just before 2 a.m. on the night of Sunday, July 1st in that year.

Before Southampton became an ocean port the American Line ships used to call each week at Plymouth to offload mails and such passengers as were anxious to reach London quickly. Such an unbalanced and occasional traffic can hardly have paid very well, but it had a prestige value, and it was hotly competed for by the Great Western and London & South Western Companies. The Great Western secured the mails, possibly because of useful connections at Bristol, but the South Western lured the passengers by exploiting its selling point of the shortest route—sixteen miles shorter than the Great Western's route at this time via Bristol. Once through Exeter the South Western had a fast road, for all that west of Salisbury the line was sharply graded.

The boat special provided was a modest five-vehicle affair. The passenger portion consisted of three standard bogie coaches converted into open firsts, sumptuously furnished but of light construction— they only weighed 23½ tons each—and calculated to give the passengers a shaking on the journey to London. The South Western track was none of the best, as we shall have cause to note in a later chapter. Together with a baggage van in front and kitchen-brake at the rear the whole set only weighed 113 tons.

The first days of the competition saw some reckless running on both sides. This was the time of City of Truro's famous run on May 9, 1904—with the mails only, no passengers aboard—when it was reputed to have reached 102·3 miles an hour down Wellington bank. That maximum (which was not dangerous) has been disputed;

not disputed is the fact that City of Truro negotiated the hills and curves between Plymouth and Newton Abbot at an average speed of nearly 57 m.p.h. To anyone who knows the road it is a performance to make the hair stand on end. The South Western took equal risks. Its road, as I have said, was a fast one; between Exeter and the London outskirts lay only a single serious impediment to speed. This was the curvature on either side of Salisbury station—on the east side, a 7½-chain reverse curve at a junction crossing leading to one of 10 chains-radius. There appears to have been no speed restriction round these curves; there was no call for one, since all expresses stopped at Salisbury. But when the boat specials started running the Exeter and Salisbury stops were cut out and Templecombe substituted as a half-way point for changing engines. In the notice laying down the specials' schedule a limit of 30 m.p.h. through Salisbury was enjoined. The limit seems to have been loosely regarded by drivers unaccustomed to mid-course restrictions and anxious to show off their paces to their newly-arrived visitors. There were stories of bribes being offered to drivers by rich Americans to bring their trains into London in record time; there was no truth in these, for the good reason that passengers had no chance to speak to the driver until arrival at Waterloo. Doubtless an occasional traveller slipped the driver a buck or two at the end of the journey and the driver told his mates; that is the sort of way rumours start. But it is possible that the knowledge of a trainload of passengers from the land of fabulous (and mostly fabled) speed records had a psychological effect.

Be that as it may, some of the speeds round the Salisbury curves were as hair-raising as anything attempted on the Great Western. Only a week or two before City of Truro's run, on April 23, 1904, that early recorder Rous-Marten had clocked a speed of 60 over the 7½-chain curve; the previous quarter-mile had been covered at 75. It was asking for trouble, but with the T9 4-4-0s generally employed —a famous and long-lived class—with their steady running and relatively low-pitched boilers, the drivers managed to get away with it.

Word of these goings-on quickly reached the ears of Dugald Drummond, that terrible old Highlander who had migrated via the North British and Caledonian Railways to spend his last years at Nine Elms, and a series of peremptory orders issued from his office:

April 20, 1904. Non-stopping trains must not pass through Salisbury at a greater speed than 30 miles an hour.

May 3, 1904. The trains must be run to scheduled time in future.

June 14, 1904. On May 3rd I requested that this train should be run to scheduled timing. Any driver running it at higher than scheduled speed will be taken off his engine.

Notice that the first order pre-dated Rous-Marten's run. It seems that even fear of 'The Governor's' wrath, which was something not lightly to be incurred, could hardly restrain the exuberance of drivers. How far these instructions affected the running through Salisbury history does not relate. It was a spot where high speed was useful to obtain impetus for the rising gradients beyond. There must still have been some speeding, for in February 1906 the schedule was altered to give a couple of extra minutes before and through Salisbury, the time being recouped beyond Basingstoke.

On the evening of June 30th the liner *New York* landed forty-three passengers at Stonehouse Pool. The boat train left Devonport at 11 p.m. on its 4 hr. 20 min. schedule to London, Templecombe stop included. Why the company should want to go tearing through the night to decant its passengers at Waterloo at the ghastly hour of 3.20 a.m. may seem passing strange, but the time of the liner's arrival would vary, and a standard schedule was laid down whatever the hour of the boat train's departure. A year or two later the Company did indeed provide sleeping cars—with real beds complete with brass knobs—in which passengers could remain until a reasonable time. But at this period, whatever the hour, the Company provided a meal. Hence the kitchen-brake at the rear, staffed by two employees of Spiers & Pond, who held the L.S.W.R. catering contract.

We turn now to the engine yard at Templecombe, where Driver Robins and Fireman Gadd were waiting to take the boat train forward. Robins was young to be a top link driver; only forty, and this was his first trip with the boat special. His engine however was not a T9, but No. 421 of the newer and larger L12 class, with boiler centre pitched 9 inches higher. The night inspector and a shunter had spoken to the engine crew, and could testify afterwards that both were sober and in good spirits. 'The boat train's running well tonight,' remarked the shunter. 'Yes,' Robins replied, 'but I shan't get into Waterloo before time, else I shall have to go up and see the Governor.'

T9 class No. 288 had made a good run from Devonport and arrived one minute early. So. No. 421 set out punctually on the 112-mile run to London, scheduled in 116 minutes, an average of nearly

58 m.p.h. Robins made no attempt to hurry at the start, and by Dinton, 20 miles out, he had dropped four minutes. Down the long falling gradients to Salisbury speed rose to something over 70—by no means an exceptional speed for this stretch. But at the approach to Salisbury Robins merely shut off steam and neglected to apply the brake. (The guard did apply it gently, but was afraid, he said, of breaking the train.) No. 421 negotiated the west curve with the whistle screaming, dashed headlong through the station and miraculously kept the rails over the reverse crossing. But on the succeeding 10-chain curve the enormous centrifugal force took effect. Helped by a 3½-inch cant the engine was not derailed, but on the left-hand curve it heeled over to the right, and the left-side wheels lifted from the rails. Even so it might have righted itself, but by evil chance a train of milk empties was passing on the down line. No. 421 struck the vans as it canted over, then overbalanced completely as it flew off at a tangent, crashed into a Beyer Peacock goods engine that was standing in the Bournemouth bay, and came to rest upon its side across the down track. The tender folded up on the engine, and the carriages piled in a heap of wreckage against the tender and the parapet of the Fisherton Street bridge. The first three vehicles were destroyed and the fourth had its side torn off; only the kitchen-brake at the rear escaped serious damage. Five vans of the milk train were also destroyed. The only horror that was not added was fire. It started, but was quickly extinguished by jets from the town hydrants.

Twenty-eight people lost their lives in the accident. Twenty-four of these were passengers, while none of the remainder escaped injury. The driver and fireman were crushed between engine and tender, and their bodies were recovered horribly mutilated. The guard of the milk train was also killed, and the fireman of the goods engine died from his injuries. Its driver was badly scalded by escaping steam.

Apart from one Englishman—a butler—and two Canadians all the dead were Americans. Many of them had to be identified by the purser and the ship's doctor of the *New York*. Queen Alexandra sent a message of sympathy to the American Ambassador, and a memorial service was held in St Paul's Cathedral. It was many years before the United States again became so involved in a British railway accident, and then in a very different capacity.

Why did Driver Robins speed to his destruction? The Inspecting Officer, Major Pringle, found his recklessness inexplicable. The Inspector recommended that the 30 m.p.h. restriction round the east curves should be reduced to 15—a recommendation which had no bearing on the cause of the accident. More to the point was a suggestion that the distant signals at Salisbury should be kept at danger, to remind drivers of the restriction.

The Company solved the problem another way. Immediately after the accident the Templecombe stop was abolished; the boat trains changed engines at Exeter and Salisbury just like the ordinary expresses, and 14 minutes were added to the schedule.

As always after a mysterious disaster, rumours started. On this very day, July 1, 1906, the Great Western had opened its direct route via Castle Cary and put an end to the South Western's distance advantage. This was enough to start the story that Robins had been tipped off to 'show 'em'. His remark at Templecombe, and his leisurely start, firmly discount this. Nor, as some believed at the time, could it be supposed that he had mistaken his whereabouts. His whistling as he approached the station showed that he was alert and knew exactly where he was.

It seems to me that this adds up to a perfectly rational explanation: Robins simply did not realize the risk he was running. He had never passed through Salisbury without stopping before, so that he had no experience of a severe restriction in the middle of a high-speed stretch. Maybe too he had heard stories of other drivers' speed exploits with the T9s. But that extra 9 inches in the centre of gravity caused him to overdo it—just. Only just, because it was calculated afterwards that to cause the engine to overturn on that curve would require a speed of at least 67 m.p.h.

Or was this an error of judgement on the part of a tired man? Robins had been on duty for 9½ hours at the time of the accident, and would have had to continue for at least a couple of hours more. Such was the railwayman's lot in the railways' heyday.

Despite its damaged state, No. 421 was run on its own wheels to Nine Elms. It remained at work for many years, and was the first engine of its class to be superheated in 1915.

In the early years of the century there was deep suspicion of high railway speeds, much as there is in some quarters against speed on the roads today, and the accident caused widespread alarm. In the House of Commons Mr Wardle, the Member for Stockport, asked the President of the Board of Trade, Mr Lloyd George, whether he would cause special enquiries to be made regarding (1) the practice of running expresses at such high speeds (hear, hear), (2) the state of the permanent ways (*sic*) and (3) the construction of the engines and other cognate matters, with a view to the prevention of such accidents. Like some people at the present day, the good Member was confusing high speed with recklessness.

But I award the palm for inspired nescience to a certain Canon Bankes, who preached the sermon at the local memorial service in Salisbury Cathedral. Many a train, he told his hearers, had passed that curve, at the same pace probably, without a hurt occurring.

The Canon was nearer the mark than he knew.

CHAPTER 3

GRANTHAM
GREAT NORTHERN RAILWAY

It happened at Salisbury; less than three months later it happened again at Grantham. On the night of September 19, 1906, the East Coast Mail, which had left Kings Cross at 8.45 p.m. and was due to stop at Grantham, ran through the station at speed and was derailed at the far end, where the points were set for the Nottingham branch.

There was a reasonable explanation at Salisbury; there was none at Grantham. How an experienced driver, who knew the road intimately and had worked this same turn only the night before, could go careering to destruction in this fashion was a mystery which sorely perplexed our grandfathers. Grantham has been called the railway equivalent of the *Marie Celeste*.[1]

Though a country town of only 24,000 inhabitants, Grantham is an important junction and was the Great Northern's principal staging point on its route to the North. Most expresses stopped there, and nearly all those that did so changed engines. The 8.45 was an exception; it formed the last leg of a Doncaster-York-Peterborough-Doncaster turn. Nevertheless the habit of engine-changing almost certainly had a bearing on the accident, as I shall show.

Let me explain the geography at Grantham. Immediately beyond the north end of the platform the Nottingham branch diverges to the left, then keeps the main line company for some distance before veering away westwards. The actual junction curve is therefore a reverse one. The engine sheds, now demolished, were on the same side of the line, and to reach them required a run up the branch and a back shunt into the engine yard. It was the custom therefore, when an express stopped, to have the points ready set for the off-going engine to run onto the branch.

The 8.45 was first and foremost a mail and parcels train; its arrival times in the North were hardly such as to attract many passengers.

[1] L.T.C. Rolt.

On this night, of its twelve-coach load only five were passenger vehicles, including two sleeping-cars, occupied by no more than about fifty travellers. It was indeed fortunate that the train was not better filled.

Awaiting the Mail at Peterborough was No. 276, one of the Ivatt large-boilered Atlantics, at that time only two years old. Driver Fleetwood on the footplate had had charge of her ever since she was built—one engine, one driver was still the rule. His regular fireman was off sick, but deputizing was a very competent young man named Talbot, who had been a premium apprentice at Doncaster and was now gaining road experience. A capable pair, and railway staff who spoke to them at Peterborough could testify that both were sober and in every way normal.

At Grantham it was nearly 11 o'clock, the time when the Mail was due. It was a dark night with occasional rain, which had made the rails greasy, but perfectly clear. Signalman Day in the South box had just passed a goods train from Leicester, coming down from the Nottingham branch, on to the up main line. That meant, of course, crossing the down main line, and Day had set the down points for the branch—as a safety precaution, it was explained afterwards. If so, it was an unnecessary one, as the goods was fully protected by the signals. Having set the points thus, Day left them there; this, it was stated at the inquiry, was in accordance with the regulations.

No. 276 should have whistled as she approached the station, but on this night there was no whistle. The next thing Day saw was that the train was passing his box—not at a moderate speed, in readiness for the stop, but at something like 60 m.p.h. The surprised signalman just had time to catch a glimpse of the men on the footplate—the only man at Grantham to do so—and could say afterwards that both appeared to be standing motionless, one on either side, each staring through his spectacle glass.

Guard Knighton, the front guard of the express, had noticed that his train had not slowed down. As he passed the South box he opened his window and found the train still travelling, as he put it, at a terrific pace. He seized the brake handle, but there was no vacuum. It would seem that the driver had applied the brakes only the moment before.

On the platform were a few intending passengers and a group of postmen waiting to load the mails. They saw the approaching head-lights nearing them a great deal faster than they should. 'It's a run through,' said one. 'No it isn't, it's got our mail carriage on it,' replied another, as the train rushed past—so fast, according to one waiting passenger, that the current of air swept parcels off a barrow on the platform. One of the postmen, Cecil Cox, noticed sparks coming from the wheels, as if the brakes had been applied. So far as he could observe in a fleeting moment, steam had been shut off. Other observers would be found to say that the brakes had not been applied, and the engine was too badly damaged for the brake handle to supply the answer. But it seems to me that Guard Knighton's evidence, taken with Cox's, is conclusive.

A few moments of horrified silence, then a noise like an explosion, and a sheet of flame lit the night sky to the north of the station. The Atlantic, with its short fixed wheelbase, had ridden the reverse curve on to the branch, but the tender became derailed and swept away the parapet of the Harlaxton Road underbridge. It then broke away and plunged down the 30-foot embankment. In doing so it derailed the engine, which slewed broadside across the tracks. The front three vehicles—mercifully all vans—piled up against the engine; the next six followed the tender down the embankment, and only the last three remained on the rails undamaged. Fire broke out in the wreckage both above and below, caused above by coals from the engine and below by escaping gas, but there are no records of any charred bodies. The driver and fireman were killed instantly; eleven of the modest complement of passengers died, as well as a postal sorter.

Why? Let us first examine the question of the points. If these had been set for the main line the express would have continued harmlessly on its way until sooner or later it was brought to a standstill. Yet this so-say safety measure steered it to its destruction. There is no proof, but I strongly suspect that the safety claim, made by the Superintendent of the Running Department, was no more than a cover-up for a slightly risky method of working, which as I have explained was to set the points for the Nottingham branch ready for the off-coming engine. It was risky, because any driver who misjudged his stop—and such things have been known to happen, especially as here on a falling gradient—would have been deflected on to the sharp curve. The Mail was the exceptional case in which engines were not changed, but the normal procedure was followed. It is significant, I think, that the Great Northern's Chief Traffic Manager, Mr W. J. Grinling, in his first announcement about the accident, stated—incorrectly of course—that the points had been set in order to change engines. However that may be, it is a fact that after the accident the working at Grantham was changed, and the points were kept set for the main line until the train had come to a stop.

But why did the driver overshoot the mark like this? A favourite theory, cherished in my own fervently teetotal home, was that he was drunk. Other rumours said that he had gone mad, or had been seen fighting with the fireman on the footplate. A less far-fetched but still unlikely explanation is that the driver was suddenly taken ill, and that the fireman's attention was diverted in attending to him. Certainly in the previous June he had been taken ill on the footplate—with sciatica, as he said—but he had been able to complete his journey and had returned to duty after a week. In any case Signalman Day's evidence would seem to dispose of the illness theory.

A *Marie Celeste* among railway accidents? Perhaps we understand these things better today, when we have become a nation of drivers. Every car driver knows how hard it is to maintain a hundred per cent concentration all the time; how easy to fall into a kind of trance. Time and again we read of some driver with a long unblemished record coming before the Courts by reason of some momentary lapse of attention. Something of the same sort, it seems to me, must have happened to Driver Fleetwood. In plain terms, his mind had wandered, and the fact that he failed to whistle seems to support this. Indeed I have seen the same thing myself, when the train I was waiting to join sailed majestically through the station—the driver had forgotten to stop. In Fleetwood's case I believe he recovered his wits as he found himself abreast of the platform, but it was then too late to avert disaster.

But what of the fireman? He was perfectly capable of stopping the train. Surely two men's minds could not have wandered simultaneously? Here I think there is a simple explanation. The fireman is nearly always—as in this case—a much younger man. Express driver is—or was—a prestigious job, and it would be a very brave or self-possessed fireman who would dare to question his senior's judgement, at all events until the last moment, when it would probably be too late. There is a case on record of a driver who toppled to his death where a bridge had been removed, because his fireman was terrified to tell him that he was on the wrong line.

No questions were asked in the House about the Grantham accident, for the good reason that the House was not sitting. But as illustrating the public ignorance of railway affairs at that time I must quote a letter from one C. J. Welton, which appeared in the *Nottingham Guardian* three days after the disaster. The writer claimed to put in 1000 miles a month on the Great Northern, and to have travelled 'hundreds of times' by this particular train. He spoke of 'this dangerous part of the journey; three or four miles on either side of the tunnel' (i.e. Stoke).

'In my humble judgement,' he went on, 'the trains go a great deal too fast. Many a time I have been thoroughly unnerved at the rate we have been travelling and felt delighted when we landed safely in Grantham station. Some of the drivers go down these steep inclines' —1 in 200 on the Grantham side—'quite steadily, apparently with the break (*sic*) on all the way. Others I can only describe as going in a mad rush. . . . If greater care were adopted by the drivers of the fast trains at curves and steep inclines, a great many valuable lives might be saved, and much misery avoided.'

Could such a comment be made today? It is an interesting speculation.

CHAPTER 4

ELLIOT JUNCTION
NORTH BRITISH & CALEDONIAN RAILWAYS

The year 1906 was a bad one for the railways. Before it was out they suffered yet a third major calamity, this time in Scotland. On December 28th, twenty-seven years to the day after the Tay Bridge disaster and less than twenty miles away, a North British train ran into the rear of a stationary Caledonian train at Elliot Junction, just over a mile south of Arbroath. It is the only accident in this book involving the passenger trains of two of the former Companies.

The Dundee to Arbroath line had been absorbed into the Caledonian, but as the North British began to push northward it was vested in joint ownership, and indeed it formed part of the North British Company's East Coast main line. The trains were staffed by the owning Companies, but for the rest the line was operated as a separate concern. Perhaps because the North British and Caledonian were not on good terms it appeared to be nobody's baby, and it was not a well-managed line.

Let us set the scene. Arbroath station in those days had no refreshment room, but the deficiency was made good by a public house known as the Victoria Bar, which stood directly opposite the station entrance on the up platform and in that pre-World War I era was open throughout the day. It is there still, and as we shall see, it figures in our story. Elliot Junction, a single island platform, was the diverging point of the now-closed Carmylie branch. In those days it was far from any habitation, and the shelterless links offered no protection from the winds which howl in from the North Sea. It would be hard to imagine a bleaker spot in winter.

The winter of 1906-7 set in early, and by the last week in December the whole of northern Europe was icebound. There were 10 degrees of frost in North-East Scotland, accompanied by snow and gales. To quote the *Scotsman*:

'Wires hung in the air from the posts like cables of ice of the thickness of one's wrist, anon poles were uprooted and crashed to the ground before the biting blast.'

In these conditions the 7.35 a.m. left Edinburgh Waverley for Aberdeen, hauled by 4-4-0 No. 324 of the 317 class, Holmes' last design. The train was in the charge of Driver Gourlay, one of the senior Haymarket drivers, who had twice driven Royalty, one of the occasions being a special for the Kaiser. In the circumstances the train did well to reach Arbroath at 10.41, about an hour late. Part of the delay was caused by a mishap earlier that morning to a south-bound goods train, which broke into three parts at Downie siding, a mile south of Elliot Junction. When this was discovered at Easthaven, two miles further on, the driver conceived the notion of returning to Elliot Junction and propelling the broken portions on to Easthaven. Not unnaturally, in the snow, the wagons were promptly derailed, and this had caused single line working between Easthaven and Elliot Junction.

This single line working was not known at Arbroath until the afternoon. All the lines were down, and no one had thought to send a messenger. So the pilotman, Inspector Souter, was provided with no pilot engine to carry him back and forth; he had to do the three miles on foot.

Arrived at Arbroath, the express came to a full stop. Both lines to the north—the North British to Montrose and the Caledonian to Forfar—were blocked; there were said to be six trains stuck in the snow. For over four hours the express hung about Arbroath station, while the stationmaster was hoping to be able to send it on. Where it waited is not quite clear, but it would seem to have been shunted onto the up platform—very handy for the Victoria Bar. There is another uncertainty. The 7.35 from Waverley was followed by the 9.35, which reached Arbroath about one o'clock, after which nothing more is heard of it. Was this the train that got in the way and prevented No. 324 from reaching the turntable?

It was now about 3 o'clock, still snowing hard, and the passengers were growing restive. They saw no prospect of reaching their destination, and began to importune the stationmaster to send the train back to Edinburgh. This he finally agreed to do. Meanwhile a Caledonian local, which had come up earlier from Dundee, was sent off from the down platform at 3.10 with fifty or so passengers.

No. 324 was still on its train facing north. It ought to have been turned for the return journey, for a long tender-first run, especially in such weather, was undesirable for every reason. But it was not turned. The turntable was awkwardly placed at St Vigean's Junction, half a mile or more to the north, and it was said that the points were blocked, or that there were coaches on the down line. The shed fore-man at St Vigean's maintained that the engine could have been turned, and as was pointed out at the inquiry, if the down line was blocked the engine could have been sent along the up line. Driver Gourlay, when he got back to Edinburgh that night and was inter-viewed by the press, maintained that the turntable was too small to take his engine, which was certainly not the case. In any case he never asked to have it turned; he knew it would be no good, he said. It looks as if the decision to return was made at short notice, and nobody really bothered about which way the engine was to travel. Tender-first running was so common on the Joint Line (the Cale-donian train had come up that way) that even in these conditions it did not seem out of place.

So Gourlay and his passengers set out on their return journey, as an all-stations train this time. Since the block telegraph system was out of action the time interval system had been introduced, and the Caledonian train was given a 16-minute start. At Arbroath South Signalman James Beattie came down from his box and told Gourlay to 'take care of himself'—a common phrase, it was explained, to use for warning drivers to go slowly and with due caution. Both Gourlay and the front guard Kinnear had already been warned to the same effect by the stationmaster. The single-line working beyond Elliot Junction was still not known at Arbroath.

The first quarter-mile or so out of Arbroath is in cutting, which offered comparative shelter. From it the train emerged to face the full fury of the storm. The plight of the enginemen, with snow driving into the cab, coal dust being whipped up by the wind and lumps of coal blown on to the footplate, can be imagined. As for Guard Kinnear, his window immediately became blocked by snow, and any lookout was impossible.

Meanwhile the Caledonian train had been held up at Elliot Junc-tion, waiting for Souter to foot it back from Easthaven. Carnegie the stationmaster at length decided that it would be safer to have the train drawn forward, while the passengers would be warmer in the waiting room. He had just decided to get them out when No. 324 appeared out of the storm travelling at about 30 m.p.h. and crashed into the rear of the waiting train. The latter's last three coaches were wrecked, as was the front coach of the North British train. No. 324 mounted the debris and fell over on her side, her driving wheels revolving furiously for ten minutes until Ogilvie, the Caledonian driver, crawled into the cab and shut the regulator. He also extricated Gourlay, who was buried in coal but not badly injured. The fireman, however, though he was rescued after seven hours, died.

Besides the fireman, twenty-one passengers were killed. Among them was an M.P., Mr. A. W. Black, Member for Banffshire, who died in hospital.

It was in character that the Joint Line should have no proper breakdown equipment, and lifting operations had to wait until Messrs Shanks' Foundry in Arbroath could send some 8-ton jacks to the scene. The breakdown train did not arrive until the early hours of the following morning.

The injured passengers were taken into the waiting room. As a sidelight on travelling conditions before train-heating became general, we read that the uninjured passengers placed rugs, wraps and other articles at the disposal of the casualties.

Quite clearly Gourlay was at fault. He maintained that the Elliot Junction home signal had given him a false clear, but after the accident it was found to be drooping only 10 degrees under the weight of the snow on the wire. Gourlay had to agree too that if, working under the caution system, the signal was at clear, it would mean that something had gone wrong. With better reason he claimed that there should have been a fogman out at the Elliot Junction distant. But in any event his speed in those conditions was reckless. It transpired that while waiting at Arbroath a passenger had taken him into the Victoria Bar, and his behaviour after the accident had seemed peculiar. He was arrested and charged with 'Culpably and recklessly driving his train while under the influence of drink'. He spent several days in the cells at Dundee before being released on £300 bail.

Since Gourlay's case was *sub judice*, the Inspecting Officer, Major Pringle, very properly decided to hold the Board of Trade inquiry in private. But the accident had caused a stir in Scotland, and the decision caused an outcry. In England the Coroner's inquest would have provided the necessary publicity, but there are no Coroners or inquests in Scotland. The *Scotsman* poured the vials of its wrath on the responsible Minister, the hated Lloyd George:

'Mr Lloyd George is probably seeking rest and relaxation after the violent sectarian agitation which has absorbed his time and ability during the winter session.'

Or again:

'Mr Lloyd George is an active and eager politician, but has shown himself less alert and efficient as an administrator.'

However the maligned Liberal Government had recently passed the Fatal Accidents Act, which was designed to fill in for Scotland the gap left by the lack of an inquest procedure. This provided for a public inquiry before a specially-convened court with a jury. Under pressure of public opinion the Lord Advocate invoked the Act, and the inquiry was held in the Arbroath Sheriff Court. Two questions engrossed the Court's attention: first, was the driver drunk? and second, ought there to have been a fogman at the Elliot Junction distant?

With regard to the first the evidence was conflicting. A parcels clerk who had gone onto the footplate about 2.30 testified to seeing Gourlay leaning out of the cab window as if he were vomiting. He added that Gourlay's speech was thick. A doctor and a police sergeant who saw Gourlay after the accident affirmed that he appeared to be drunk. Other witnesses declared with equal emphasis that he appeared shocked, but certainly not drunk. Gourlay himself said that he had had just one nip (small whisky) with a passenger in the Victoria Bar and had come straight out. He had refused a glass (a double) and also a flask of something which a passenger offered him on the footplate.

The fogman question resolved itself into a contest between the North British Railway, as Gourlay's employer, and the Joint Line, which was responsible for the signalling. The Joint Line's lawyer questioned Mr M'Clellan, the N.B.R. Traffic Inspector from Edinburgh: 'Do you think it reasonable', he asked, 'to have kept a fogman at that signal, with no trains from 9 a.m. to 3.30?' 'I know he would have been kept on the North British line,' came the reply. M'Clellan had been at Arbroath on the day of the accident. 'I have never known a greater need for fog signalling in all my experience,' he declared. He had nothing to do with the Joint Line, he was at pains to explain, but he had heard that it hardly ever used fog signals. Gourlay had had them at Easthaven going down, but that appeared to be the exceptional case. It was stated that since the accident fog signals had been introduced—sufficient admission of the previous negligence.

Predictably, the jury found that Gourlay was at fault in not obeying his instructions to go carefully. Nothing was said about his being drunk. The jury also found that fog signals should have been used. They added that the North British train should have been held up longer.

The evidence at the inquiry, and the jury's findings, had evidently made the police think again about the charge of drunkenness, and when Gourlay came to stand his trial the indictment had been altered. It now read that: He failed to proceed cautiously, failed to bring his engine to a stand at Elliot Junction signal box . . . and so caused his train and engine to collide and killed the twenty-two named persons. He was found guilty by a majority verdict of ten to five and sentenced to five months' imprisonment, but the sentence was remitted.

In his report to the Board of Trade Major Pringle brushed aside Gourlay's story of the single nip. He held that:

'The lack of intelligence, or of caution and alertness, displayed by Driver Gourlay were in part, at all events, induced by drink, the effects of which may possibly have been accentuated after he left Arbroath by exposure to the weather.'

He added the following passage, which reads oddly today:

'I have to point out that the proximity of the Victoria Bar to the up platform is a very undesirable feature of the surroundings of the station. The substitution of a coffee shop and refreshment room would be greatly in the general interests of the staff.'

The Inspector roundly condemned the goods driver's idea of propelling wagons through the snow as sheer folly and bound to lead to a derailment. He had a number of unflattering things to say about operational methods on the Joint Line. If the staff at Arbroath, he pointed out, had been told of the single-line working Gourlay could have been warned of the possible hold-up of the Caledonian train.

Gourlay is still remembered at Arbroath; station staff there to whom I spoke could recall his name straightaway. Elliot Junction is no longer in the wilds; the Arbroath Industrial Estate is next door and a caravan site has grown up just opposite. But on the shore side the links are as desolate as ever, except for summer picnic parties.

I end this account with a reminiscence. In September of that same year, 1907, I was staying with my family on a farm in Berwickshire, close to which ran the East Coast line. I was watching the trains one day with my father, a Scotsman and an early railfan, when No. 324 passed, travelling light. 'Hullo,' said my father, 'that's the engine that was in the Arbroath accident.' So I first came to hear of the accident that was to be known as Elliot Junction.

CHAPTER 5

SHREWSBURY

LONDON & NORTH WESTERN RAILWAY

Salisbury, Grantham, and now, just over a year later, Shrewsbury. For yet a third time a night express became derailed on a curve by a station, killing both enginemen and many others. At Shrewsbury the curve was at the entrance to the station instead of beyond it as in the other two cases, but otherwise the circumstances were almost identical. It happened on October 15, 1907, at just after two o'clock in the morning.

On this night the West of England Mail due out of Crewe at 1.20 had its usual motley collection of vehicles—North Western, Great Western, W.C.J.S. and one Caledonian covered truck—drawn from Scotland, Liverpool and York. Of its fifteen vehicles only five were passenger carriages, of which three, all Great Western, were marshalled at Nos. 2, 3 and 4. Despite its length it was by L.N.W.R. standards not a heavy train : 287 tons, and as usual with night mail trains it carried a fairly light passenger complement of about seventy. At the head was 'Experiment' class No. 2052, 'Stephenson', which had only entered service in January of the same year. Like most cross-country runs, the schedule to Shrewsbury was an easy one—$32\frac{1}{2}$ miles in 45 minutes.

We must now take a look at the driver, and speculate whether his personality might have had anything to do with the accident. Driver Martin, who was fifty-two, comes across to us as a bit of a bad lad. He was a big man of fourteen stone and fond of his pint, though it was proved that on this night he had not been drinking. His record as a driver was anything but unblemished. He had thirteen entries against his name (two of them while still a fireman) : five for absence without leave or missing his train, four for running past stations where he was due to stop, two for overrunning signals at danger, one for dropping seventeen minutes without cause and one for emitting black smoke at a station. His various failures to stop at stations, including such a sizeable one as Wilmslow, he attributed in each case to misreading the Working Time Book. All of which, in the Inspecting Officer's words, 'indicate, to put it mildly, an occasional lack of attention on Martin's part to his duties.'

Fireman Fletcher by contrast, who was twenty-nine, emerges as a quite saintly young man, 'of a steady, sober, thrifty nature', and a strict teetotaller. He had never fired for Martin before.

Should we be right to regard Martin as accident-prone, as the phrase goes these days? Not exactly, perhaps, but he was hardly the man to show that extra alertness and resistance to fatigue which are demanded by night driving.

Martin and Fletcher, both Crewe men, had come on duty at Holyhead at about 7.30 that evening. They had booked off there at six o'clock the previous morning, and had therefore had over 12 hours' rest. They had spent the day in the Holyhead enginemen's hostel, as the Company's rules demanded. Their turn of duty was not an arduous one: the 8.50 parcels to Crewe, a couple of hours there doing odd shunting jobs, then the run to Shrewsbury and back to Crewe—a total mileage of 170, hardly a diagram to satisfy the running department today.

The 1.20 left Crewe eight minutes late and dropped a couple more minutes before passing Whitchurch. From that point it covered the 18¾ miles in nineteen minutes, five minutes under the generous schedule time. The approach to Shrewsbury is down three miles of falling gradients, of which the steepest part, known as Battlefield Bank, consists of two miles at 1 in 117. At the foot of the bank is Crewe Bank signal box, 600 yards from the junction with the Great Western line from Chester, into which the North Western line converges almost at the platform end by means of a curve of about nine chains radius. The junction is controlled by a second box, Crew Junction. Shrewsbury station has only three through platforms, of which the centre one is used for two-way working. It sometimes happens therefore that a train has to wait outside the station until a platform is clear for it. So it was on this night. When Crewe Bank offered the train to the Junction box the latter accepted it under the Section Clear But Station Blocked signal, which meant that the signalman at Crewe Bank must stop the train and caution the driver. The signalman had therefore kept his signals at danger. But instead of stopping, the train came careering down the bank and passed his box at a high speed. He immediately sent the 4-5-5 signal, Train Running Away on Right Line, to Crewe Junction, but before he had finished transmitting his fourteen rings the train had reached the junction curve at a speed estimated at fully 60 m.p.h.

Without too great a flight of fancy we can picture those last moments on 'Stephenson's' footplate. Martin has dozed off, his hand still on the regulator handle, which keeps him upright. Fletcher has not noticed that his driver is asleep, for he is busy filling the boiler and putting his fire in order ready for coming off at Shrewsbury. Suddenly Martin wakes up, or Fletcher wakes him; they see the Crewe Bank home signal at danger and realize that they are at the bottom of the incline and travelling much too fast to be able to pull up for the junction curve. At this moment they would probably be doing not less than 75 m.p.h., for the Experiment class, despite their smallish 6 feet 3 inches coupled wheels, were free-running engines downhill. Desperately Martin applies the brake and puts his engine into reverse, while he also manages to sound a series of warning blasts on the whistle. But all is of little avail to reduce speed much in the distance. There comes the moment of horror when 'Stephenson' turns over, then oblivion. Very probably a similar scene had been enacted at Grantham.

'Stephenson' had struck the facing points where the junction splays out at the approach to the platform. Its wheels being suddenly deflected to the left, the effect was the same as at Salisbury. The engine keeled over on its right, skidded for a distance and came to rest on its side some twenty or thirty yards from the platform end. The first two vehicles were totally destroyed; the third was thrown aside and landed on the Great Western track twenty yards away, while the next six coaches piled up in a heap behind the engine. Eighteen lives were lost: eleven passengers, two guards, three post office sorters, besides the driver and fireman.

Notice the two guards killed. It is a commentary on railway working in those days that there were no less than five guards on the train, and one may ask why none of them managed to stop it. The answer is surely much the same as the one I suggested at Grantham in regard to the fireman: that no guard would be likely to take action until he was quite sure that the driver had failed to do so, when it would almost certainly be too late. At least one guard, named Birch, did try to stop the train. Noticing the excessive speed as it passed Crewe

Bank box he moved to apply the brake, but found that the driver had already done so.

This third accident in the 'runaway' series caused considerable public commotion, and on the first day of the inquiry Mr Lloyd George himself, still President of the Board of Trade, took his seat beside the Inspecting Officer, Col. Yorke. He questioned the Crewe locomotive foreman closely about Martin's hours of duty. His questions were not unreasonable, for at that time, long before the introduction of the eight-hour day, railwaymen were not seldom called upon to work excessive hours. Martin's hours had not been excessive, but he had been out of bed for the whole of four out of the previous six nights, and several letters to the Inspector from retired enginemen put their finger on the spot. They gave personal experiences of going to sleep for a few minutes on the footplate; often, they pointed out, drivers did not manage to get proper sleep during daytime rests. It is the same trouble that afflicts nurses and others who have to do intermittent night work. Indeed a fireman, writing many years ago in the *Railway Magazine*, said that he would prefer to work permanently on nights rather than turn about, for this reason.

There was no other possible explanation. The unfortunate Martin's organs were dispatched to London and subjected to a rigorous analysis, which conclusively ruled out any possibility of a seizure or sudden illness. It also showed that he had had nothing to eat or drink for some hours before the accident; no trace of alcohol was found.

The engine 'Stephenson', as I have said, belonged to the Experiment class. The prototype, No. 66 'Experiment' had simply taken the name and number of Webb's pioneer 3-cylinder compound, which was very definitely an experiment and a highly unsuccessful one. But to the uninitiated the name sounded suspicious, especially when, as in the *Shrewsbury Chronicle*, 'Stephenson' was described as belonging to a type 'known as the six-wheeled coupled experiment class'. What? said the journalists. Entrust an important express to an experimental engine? Disgraceful. The press seems to have had a field day over Shrewsbury. The type of article can be gauged from the following comment by the pundit Rous-Marten:

'The usual ill-informed nonsense has pervaded many of the non-technical journals alike in London and in the provinces. It is broadly asserted that the driver was travelling at "excessive speed" in order to make up time, as he had started late from Crewe. And it is even implied that the poor driver went mad under the mental strain and anxiety involved in the compulsion placed upon him to run at a reckless and dangerous rate with this object in view. Was there ever such flaring flapdoodle, such blatant bosh?"[1]

Rous-Marten had a nice line in alliteratives, but the press was onto a first-rate mystery story. However Shrewsbury was the last of its kind. With it the sequence of midnight runaways came to an end, never to be repeated.

[1] *Railway Magazine*, December 1907.

CHAPTER 6

HAWES JUNCTION
MIDLAND RAILWAY

The Settle and Carlisle line of the old Midland Company is not only the finest piece of railway engineering in Britain; it offers unequalled railway panoramas for those who are prepared to climb. I have stood on the summit of Whernside and watched three goods trains chasing each other up the Long Drag to Blea Moor; I have sat with my feet dangling over the scarp of Wild Boar Fell, whence I could almost have dropped a stone on to the toy trains at Ais Gill, nearly 1200 feet below. I have followed the course of the Thames-Clyde Express for many miles as it made its way up the Eden valley, only to be brought to a stand at Mallerstang box by a laggard goods which ought to have been shunted at Kirkby Stephen.

Enough of reminiscing! This grim but glorious country was the scene, within three years and about two miles of each other, of the two worst disasters in the history of the Midland Railway. The first occurred in the early hours of Christmas Eve, 1910, about one and a half miles north of Hawes Junction, the station now known as Garsdale. Though the immediate cause was a signalman's forgetfulness, it was indirectly due to the Midland Company's small engine policy.

Throughout its history the Midland built nothing bigger than sixty-ton 4-4-0s for its express trains or fifty-ton 0-6-0s for goods. While all its neighbours were using eight-coupled engines it handled its vast coal traffic to London with 0-6-0s working in pairs. For passenger trains rigid load limits were laid down for each class of engine, above which a pilot had to be taken, which was frequently. Such prodigal methods were made possible by booming business and low wages.

On the Settle and Carlisle line this meant that all expresses above a moderate weight had to be piloted up to the summit at Ais Gill, 1169 feet above sea level; southbound from Carlisle, forty-eight miles away, and northbound from either Hellifield or Leeds, the latter sixty-four miles distant. The pilot engines were turned at Hawes

Junction, three miles south of Ais Gill, to return to their home shed light. When traffic wâs heavy, as at holiday times, it meant that Hawes Junction was a busy place.

So it was on this Christmas Eve. It was a pitch black night and raining as it so often does in the High Pennines—a drenching downpour of fine rain. Whipped by a north-west gale, this was driving against the windows of the signal box, where Signalman Sutton was having to cope with no less than nine light engines, which had arrived from Ais Gill during the previous hour in strings of four, three and two. The two Carlisle engines, Nos. 448 and 548, were Class 2 rebuilds; the remainder, bound for Hellifield or Leeds, were a fine typical bunch of ancient Midland locomotive power, including four unrebuilt 4-4-0s of 1877 vintage, a whole clutch of which had come to roost at Hellifield.

The time was 5.20 a.m.; Sutton had been on duty since eight o'clock the previous evening and was due to be relieved at six. The two Carlisle engines had been turned on the famous stockaded turntable—the only one in Britain to have to be protected from the wind by a fence. At this moment they were waiting on the back platform —the one used by the North Eastern trains from Northallerton— for a down excursion to pass. Meanwhile two of the Leeds engines were turned ready to move off, and a Hellifield engine, 4-4-0 No. 312, ran up to the turntable.

The excursion ran through. As soon as it was clear Sutton moved the Carlisle engines across to the advance starting signal on the main line. He could have dispatched them as soon as the excursion had passed Ais Gill, and no doubt he intended to do so. But he was preoccupied meanwhile with the up line, on which two fast goods trains were due, and with getting away the light engines for Leeds. The two goods trains ran through at 5.20 and 5.43, after which Sutton dispatched the two Leeds engines.

By this time the two Carlisle engines had gone out of Sutton's mind. He should have been reminded of them by one or other of the firemen under Rule 55, which instructs a driver waiting at a signal to send his guard or fireman to the signal box. The rule was devised for out-of-course situations, and at Hawes Junction it was normal practice for returning light engines to run up to the down advance starter behind an express that had just passed. They never had to wait more than four to six minutes, the time that it took for an express to clear

Ais Gill. It was thought unnecessary to carry out an emergency procedure for a regular operation, especially as the engines were in full view of the signal box. So at Hawes Junction light engines did not observe the rule. Drivers Scott and Bath in charge of Nos. 448 and 548 were expecting to be sent off at any moment.

Meanwhile at 5.39 the midnight express from St Pancras had been offered from Dent. It had carried a fairly full load as far as Leeds, but there were only fifty-six left to go forward, including seventeen in the sleeping cars. Because its weight of 207 tons was twenty-seven tons over the unpiloted limit for Class 2 No. 549 she was given a pilot, No. 48, an old Kirtley 2-4-0 which had spent its life on the Settle and Carlisle line. The express had made a special stop at Skipton, and was running sixteen minutes late. It was now travelling at about 60 m.p.h. on the lofty stretch of level that precedes the final short climb to the summit. Sutton obtained acceptance from Ais Gill and pulled off his signals. The time was 5.44.

When the advance starter came off the two drivers, who had been waiting for about twenty minutes, naturally took it for their signal. They 'popped' their whistles and moved off. Whether Sutton could have heard them in that wind, or seen them properly through his rain-bleared windows, is open to question; at all events he did neither. So he was surprised when Driver Tempest of No. 312 came into the box with a very odd look on his face.

Tempest had seen it all. He had seen the light engines run across, then wait, then move off under the express's signals. A minute or two later the express passed through, and was lost to sight in the cutting beyond. Tempest turned to his mate. 'How far have them engines got?' he asked. 'It would have taken them all their time to clear Moorcock Tunnel,' his fireman answered. He had hardly spoken when the long scream of a whistle was borne down upon the gale from the north. 'He's catched 'em,' said Tempest, and went up into the box. 'Hullo,' said Sutton, 'I intended coupling you up to the two light engines going south, but you have been longer on the turntable than I reckoned for, so I let them go.' Tempest ignored this remark. The way he looked at me, said Sutton, made me think that something was wrong. 'What have you done with those two engines?' Tempest asked. 'They've gone to Carlisle,' Sutton replied. 'They've not,' Tempest retorted. 'When you pulled off for the down express them two engines was standing on the down road behind the advance starter waiting for it to come off, and when it came off they went.'

Sutton laughed incredulously. But a look at his train register, and a call to Signalman Bellas at Ais Gill, told him what he dreaded to know. He looked out of his box to the North, where the low-hanging clouds had turned to an angry red. 'I've done it,' he said. It was now nearly 6 a.m., and Signalman Simpson, who was due to relieve Sutton, had come into the box. 'Will you go to Stationmaster Bence,' said Sutton, 'and say that I am afraid I have wrecked the Scotch express.'

Drivers Scott and Bath had got a mile or more on their way and were travelling easily at about 25 m.p.h. They were in the neighbourhood of Lunds viaduct when Bath, looking back, saw something which he could hardly believe—express headlights in the Moorcock Tunnel behind them. A moment later the express burst out of the tunnel, the engines throwing sparks high in the air as they pounded up the 1 in 165 gradient at 65 m.p.h. When he had recovered from his surprise, which it would seem he was slow in doing, Bath opened his regulator and his whistle, while Scott hearing him did the same. Driver Oldcorn of No. 48 did not see Bath's tail light at once; drifting steam and the mist-like rain, together with the obstruction of the Grisedale Crossing footbridge, obscured it from his view. So the two engines were hardly more than a hundred yards apart—say six seconds' travelling at a net speed of 40 m.p.h.—before the drivers realized the danger. It was only then that either of them took action, far too late to have much effect.

The two light engines were driven forward for several hundred yards, Bath's engine minus its bogie, before they overturned at the mouth of Shotlock Hill Tunnel. Nearly two hundred yards behind them both engines of the express went over against the side of the cutting, and the first six of its coaches followed them. The two front coaches were telescoped and completely wrecked; all the dead were in these two. Apart from the two sleeping cars, the whole train was fitted with Pintsch oil lighting, the gas being stored in cylinders beneath the coaches at a pressure which at this moment was about 80 lb. per square inch. The high pressure main pipe on the leading coach was broken, and the escaping gas was ignited by the showers of sparks from the derailed bogies and displaced brake gear. A shepherd in a cottage nearby saw a blinding flash as the gas took fire. Fanned by the strong head wind, the fire quickly enveloped the entire train.

Though dazed and badly hurt in the leg, Bath quickly picked

himself up and walked through the downpour to Ais Gill box to warn the signalman. Meanwhile Johnson 2-4-0 No. 250, which was running light tender first from Carlisle—what a journey in such weather and on a practically unprotected footplate!—had passed Ais Gill at 5.55, seven minutes after the accident. Driver Judd noticed nothing as he approached the scene, for the fire had not yet appeared on the surface of the wreckage, but Oldcorn managed to attract his attention by sounding the whistle of the derailed No. 48. Judd halted alongside—the leftward derailment had left the up line clear—and emptied the contents of his tender on to the now flaming debris. But the fire had taken too firm a hold. Stationmaster Bence came up from Hawes Junction on an engine commandeered from a goods train; this managed to draw the two rear vans to safety, but the remaining vehicles were buffer-locked and immoveable, and were burnt out.

Let us pause here to ask the question: could the collision have been avoided, or at all events much reduced in violence? The Inspecting Officer, Major Pringle, decided that it could not have been in the prevailing conditions of visibility, and that no blame attached to any of the enginemen on this account. Perhaps we ought to accept the Inspector's verdict, and certainly in Oldcorn's case we may give him the benefit of the doubt. But what about Bath? Agreed that he merely chanced to look back and see the express. But it was then a good 500 yards behind him, and for another 400 yards—say half-a-minute at 25 m.p.h.—he did nothing about it. If he had whistled and accelerated on the instant, the two light engines might have got just that much further ahead to enable Oldcorn to brake with greater effect, and perhaps to have staved off the collision. This is the first of several occasions on which we shall have cause to wonder whether a quicker reaction by a driver might not have prevented a crash.

Twelve passengers perished in this disaster. Three of the corpses were never identified, and are buried in Hawes churchyard. I speak of corpses, but bits of corpses would be more accurate. Skin, heads, upper and lower limbs—all were totally consumed; only fragments of the trunks remained. 'Adult male, evidently of fine physique', 'adult, spinal column only, impossible to state sex', 'adult, shoulders only'—these were some of the descriptions of the charred remains which were conveyed to a temporary mortuary at the Moorcock Inn, a mile from the scene.

Major Pringle's report placed prime responsibility for the accident on Signalman Sutton, which the latter had admitted from the first.

The two light engine drivers, Scott and Bath, were also held to be gravely at fault in not carrying out Rule 55. 'I hold it is no good excuse for men to say that they were momentarily expecting the signal to fall,' wrote the Inspector. But Bath's conduct after the accident was highly commended.

The Inspector had a number of recommendations to make. On the subject of gas lighting he was surprisingly equivocal. It was pointed out that over forty years had passed since the last case of fire causing death or injury to a passenger in an accident; that was at Abergele in 1868, when two paraffin-filled trucks ran away and crashed into the Irish Mail. Gas has many advantages over electricity as a source of illumination, wrote Major Pringle, and he recommended making it safer by means of stronger cylinders and cut-off valves which would act in the event of the main pipe breaking. 'But,' he concluded, 'I still hold that electricity is the more desirable and should be adopted wherever possible.' This comparatively mild judgement brought down on him the wrath of the *Journal of Gas Lighting*, which protested against the suggestion that gas illuminant was the cause of the fire. 'It was caused by coals from the second engine of the express', claimed the writer. He also asserted that 'several accidents accompanied by the terrors of fire have occurred in electrically-lit trains, also in America'—without quoting any actual cases.

The Inspector also suggested that the Midland should use lever collars as was done by many other lines. The collar is a bright red object which is slipped over the lever to remind the signalman not to pull it, as the line is obstructed. The Midland did not hold with the use of collars, on the grounds that they made the signalman careless, and we shall come across a case—at Quintinshill—where collars were provided but were not used. But if collars had been available at Hawes Junction, and had been used, the accident would not have happened.

Lastly Major Pringle referred to another device of which we shall hear a great deal as we go on. This is the track-circuit. It was invented in America in 1872, but made no great headway in this country until the turn of the century. The principle of the track circuit is this; a section of rail is insulated at rail joints from adjoining sections. A low-voltage current is passed continuously through the rails; this operates a switch or relay which is normally maintained in the closed position. When a train enters the insulated section it short-circuits this current and opens the switch, and the train's presence is revealed by an indicator in the signal box. It will be seen that should the current fail, or an accidental short-circuit take place, the device will behave as if there were a train in the section. Any failure, that is to say, would be on the safe side, an essential feature of any protective device. Had track circuits been installed at Hawes Junction the indicator would have shown 'occupied', and the presence of the light engines would have been revealed.

The Midland Railway took the Inspector's advice about track circuiting to heart, and after the Ais Gill accident three years later was able to claim that in this respect it had more than fulfilled his recommendations, but it still did not provide lever collars, and at least one other serious accident occurred in L.M.S. days—at Hope in 1925—because of the lack of them. Nor did it discontinue its policy of building vehicles lighted by gas, preferring the Inspector's alternative recommendation of installing cut-off valves. It needed the even more terrible accident at Ais Gill to convince the Midland that gas lighting, whatever its merits, simply was not worth the risk.

CHAPTER 7

DITTON JUNCTION
LONDON & NORTH WESTERN
RAILWAY

In the unlovely countryside of south Lancashire, close to the town of Widnes, lies the station of Ditton Junction on the former North Western Crewe to Liverpool line. It was here that a holiday express became derailed as it ran through a crossover on September 17, 1912. Just as in our last accident at Hawes Junction, fire broke out, caused once again by escaping gas.

The layout at Ditton Junction is unusual, and as it was the driver's ignorance of it which caused the accident I must beg the reader's patience while I describe it. The station is approached from the east by three double lines. In the centre is the line from Crewe, descending on an embankment at a gradient of 1 in 114 from the height of the Runcorn Bridge. I will call this line the main line. Flanking it on either side are two different routes from Warrington, which I will call Warrington north and Warrington south. Warrington north does not concern us, except that its presence may have helped to confuse the driver. From Ditton the Warrington south tracks continue towards Liverpool as the slow line, while the main line becomes the fast line. But—and this is the unusual feature—from the main line to Warrington south there are two crossovers within 100 yards of each other, which I will call crossovers A and B. Crossover A, which comes first, is to enable freight trains from the Crewe line to reach a pair of goods lines which diverge from the Warrington south line at that point. Crossover B, close to the overbridge at the platform end, is where the Warrington south line becomes the slow main line; it is, in fact, the fast-to-slow line crossover. Crossover A could do duty in both capacities; the second one was doubtless added to avoid conflicting train movements. But it would be perfectly possible for a driver not well acquainted with the route to be unaware that there were two crossovers and to misread the signals that controlled them, and that is exactly what this driver did. Of course drivers are supposed to be thoroughly familiar with the roads they traverse, but on this occasion it did not happen that way.

The signals in question consisted first, of splitting distants; two signals side by side, one for the fast line and one for crossing over to the slow line via B. There was no distant for crossover A. Second, there was a gantry of three home signals, reading, right to left, main line, crossover B, crossover A. The first two carried distants underneath them for Ditton Junction No. 2 box; the crossover A signal was carried on a shorter post and had no distant. Remember that the Warrington north tracks, which had no signals at this point, were on the right of the main line. Three sets of tracks, three signals. It would be perfectly easy for a driver coming down the main line to read the centre signal as applying to himself to continue on the centre track, whereas in fact it was the fast-to-slow line signal. This is undoubtedly what the driver did. I should add that both crossovers were subject to a speed restriction of 15 m.p.h.

The 5.30 p.m. summer-only from Chester, with through coaches from Afon Wen, consisted of three six-wheelers and four eight-wheelers marshalled in that order, as well as, incongruously for a holiday express, two Great Western horse boxes next to the engine. It was hauled by the smallest engine we shall encounter actually in charge of a train—2-4-0 'Precedent' class 'Cook', weighing without its tender less than 36 tons. It seems remarkable that the L.N.W.R., which by this time was well provided with modern engines, should entrust a fast train to such an old stager, but this had no bearing on the accident. What did have a bearing was the fact that 'Cook's' leading wheels had no side play, which gave the engine a rigid wheelbase of over 15 feet. A bogie engine would probably have kept the rails, so at least the Inspecting Officer thought.

How did the train come to be entrusted to a driver so badly acquainted with the road? His name was Robert Hughes; he belonged to Llandudno Junction shed, and it is there to which we must go for the explanation. Hughes was young for a driver, only forty-one; he was in fact a spare driver who had doubtless been called upon to help out with the summer traffic. In the same way his fireman was a cleaner, eligible to go firing as required. The arranger of engines, as he was called, at Llandudno Junction was a certain Owen Owens, who was only a driver himself—'a man of no authority,' as the Inspecting Officer put it. We get a hint of easy Welsh informality—a trait which we shall encounter on a bigger scale at Abermule a few chapters further on—in Hughes' remark to Owens: 'I'm all right for Liverpool,' which Owens accepted as meaning that Hughes knew the road. Unfortunately Hughes was not all right. He had traversed the road as fireman many times, and had signed the road book as a driver four years before, but in those four years he had only driven to Liverpool on ten occasions, on none of which had he been put across from the fast to the slow line at Ditton. His experience as a fireman was worth very little, for these signals were on the left-hand side—the driver's side on the North Western—and he would not therefore have been called upon to look out for them. Hughes himself however had no misgivings. He could have called for a pilot at Chester, but did not do so.

So 'Cook' came hurtling down the gradient from Runcorn at a good 60 m.p.h., Hughes evidently believing that he was set for the straight road. So he would have been in the normal way, but it happened that a London express was close behind him, which was due to pass his train before Liverpool was reached. So the unsuspecting driver found himself switched on to the crossover. 'Cook' left the rails, turned on its side, slithered along the track still steaming and fetched up against a pier of the overbridge, from which it dislodged a quantity of brickwork. As it struck the bridge the boiler sheared away from the firebox; in fact, the engine broke its back. The leading horsebox was thrown right over the bridge and landed on the station platform beyond. The second horsebox was cut in half, and one half landed either side of the bridge. The horse was killed, but the groom escaped. The three six-wheelers formed a compact mass of wreckage under the bridge and against the wall of the booking office; no passengers in the first two coaches survived. One eight-wheeler came to rest on top of the bridge; the remaining three kept upright, but all were damaged.

The whole train was gas-lit. Fire did not break out on the instant as at Hawes Junction, but within a few minutes it began to show in the wreckage. There was a plentiful supply of water, as well as of skilled fire-fighters from the chemical works nearby, but gas-fed fires are not so easily extinguished. This one blazed for a couple of hours, and the whole fore part of the train was consumed. Driver Hughes was killed instantly; his fireman was rescued after many hours but died in hospital. Thirteen passengers also died, but their bodies were recognizable, and it was established that none of them had been burned to death.

We get a period flavour in a reporter's description of the scene on the platform:

'The charred luggage,' he wrote, 'lay in heaps, together with hats, caps, fur boas, luncheon baskets, fruit, sweets and holiday literature.'

We also read that the work of rescue was hampered by the crowd of spectators—all doubtless eager to help.

I mentioned that 'Cook' was said to have broken its back, but a photograph taken after it was re-railed gives a rather different impression. The cab and smokebox have disappeared, and the boiler looks as if it had been telescoped into the firebox. Perhaps the boiler had been roughly replaced on the frames for removal.

At the inquiry the Inspecting Officer, Col. Yorke, criticized the signalling installation. It was unnecessary and confusing, he said, to have a distant signal for one crossover and not for the other. A single distant which would stand at caution when a train was to be crossed was all that was required. If the fast-to-slow line distant were retained, it should carry on its post a speed restriction warning sign. As regards the driver's knowledge of the road the Chief Mechanical Engineer, Mr C. J. Bowen Cook, maintained that Hughes was thoroughly conversant with it, but the Inspector did not agree. Hughes should have applied for a pilot at Chester, he said.

Of all the scenes of accidents in this book, Ditton Junction is the most changed today. Everything is concrete and shiny and new, for the station is part of British Railways' showpiece, the London Midland electrification. The brick bridge with which 'Cook' tried conclusions has been replaced by one of reinforced concrete. Where the little engine came racing down the gradient to its doom the blue electrics sweep noiselessly past. The fatal crossover has been re-aligned at so gentle an angle that even 'Cook' might hope to negotiate it safely at speed. But it has no moveable diamonds, and is still subject to a 20 m.p.h. restriction. The signals which misled Hughes have disappeared, and the continuous colour lights are glimpsed beneath the overhead forest of the catenary. Most striking of all is the new push-button signal box, in which the ring of a bell is rarely heard. The young stationmaster can rightly be proud of his station.

It is interesting to consider what would happen should a latter-day Hughes chance to traverse the line. Three colour lights away he would have the first warning in the form of a double yellow. The second light would show a single yellow and the third a red. Just before he was brought to a stop the signal would show the 'feathers', a diagonal row of white lights, indicating that he was to be crossed over. Moreover at each light a hooter would sound in the cab and the brakes be automatically applied. Ditton Junction then and now is the epitome of fifty years' railway progress.

CHAPTER 8

AIS GILL

MIDLAND RAILWAY

It happened a second time. Once again the night sky over the High Pennines was lit by the glare of a burning train. No wonder the local newspaper headed its story: 'Another Hawes Disaster'. It resembled that accident in being a rear-end collision, and in the fire which followed, but the other circumstances were wholly different. It happened just after 3 a.m. on September 2, 1913. A night express from Glasgow and Stranraer had stalled on the 1 in 100 gradient about half-a-mile short of Ais Gill summit; while still standing it was run into by the following Edinburgh train, which had run through the signals at Mallerstang. The fire was less destructive than at Hawes Junction but the loss of life was greater; sixteen passengers were killed or died of injuries.

The story begins at Carlisle, where the two 4-4-0s, Class 4 No. 993 and Class 2 No. 446, were being coaled at Durran Hill shed. The coal was from a new source of supply—two small pits in the South Tyne coalfield, chosen doubtless because of the short, cheap haul to Carlisle. 'Splendid coal for the Carlisle road,' was the verdict of the Company's stores inspector, and so it may have been in calorific value. But it was small and was said to clinker easily. Moreover both collieries lacked modern screening equipment, so that truckloads were apt to turn up at Carlisle well impregnated with slack. There had been constant grumbles by engine crews during the few weeks in which the coal had been in use, though apparently no official complaints.

Thus Driver Nicholson of No. 993 was not reassured when he found that the Glasgow train loaded to 243 tons—thirteen tons above his engine's rated maximum—and he promptly asked for a pilot. Such a request would have seemed laughable on the neighbouring London & North Western line, where the George the Fifth Class, of much the same power as the Class 4s, had been known to take over 300 tons unaided up the much steeper northbound ascent to Shap. But the Midland, as we have seen, was very pilot-conscious. Unlike the North Western, it was averse to flogging its engines. It was the more surprising therefore that for once in a way a pilot was refused. There was one available, but it was reckoned that more time would be lost fetching and attaching it than Nicholson would lose to the summit unaided. So he had to tackle the climb to Ais Gill, exactly 1100 feet above the yard at Carlisle, without assistance.

For a start Nicholson did well enough. Over the first thirty-three miles to Ormside, which lies about 500 feet above sea level, the line undulates upwards, and to this point Nicholson only dropped a minute on the forty-one-minute schedule. But on the long stretches of 1 in 100 beyond speed rapidly began to fall away; the Class 4s, with their large 28 square feet grates, seemed to find more difficulty in keeping a fire with this coal than the smaller Class 2s. To Mallerstang, the last box before the summit, another eight minutes had been lost, and though Nicholson gave his fireman a hand with the shovel, pressure steadily fell. To prevent the brakes leaking on Nicholson had to keep his large ejector working—more loss of steam. Finally, just that half-mile from the summit and safety, with pressure down to 85 lb., No. 993 came to a standstill. Now to restore pressure with a bad fire is no speedy task. One day in 1951, on the other side of the hill, our 'Jubilee' panted to a standstill on Ribblehead viaduct, and there we stuck for a good half-hour before it could raise enough steam to continue. Nicholson admitted afterwards that he expected to be at least ten minutes, which sounds very much on the quick side. But he did not say to the front guard Donelly, who came to enquire the cause of the stop. 'We'll be a few minutes,' he said. 'Only a minute,' Donelly called out to the rear guard Whitley. As rear guard it was Whitley's duty to protect the train with detonators, the more so as he knew that the Edinburgh train was following, but having been told 'only a minute' he did not bother to do so. Yet he must have had a good idea what the trouble was, and that the train would be standing for much longer than that. 'I think he knew,' wrote the Inspector.

We return to Carlisle to meet the main character in our story: Samuel Caudle, driver of No. 446. He was fifty-nine, with twenty-one years' driving experience, and we discern in him one of those typically solid, capable drivers whom as a small boy I used to worship as heroes. A bit on the slow side, perhaps, and not blessed with over-much imagination. His record was a splendid one, and included seven awards for vigilance. His fireman, Follows, was new to him, and what was no less pertinent, new to the engine. It was a circumstance which undoubtedly had a bearing on the accident.

Caudle had made his protest against the coal before leaving the shed. 'If she'll steam on this, she'll steam on anything', he had remarked. But he had no claim to a pilot. His load was a typical Midland featherweight—six coaches totalling only 157 tons, twenty-three tons below the maximum allowed to the moderately-powered Class 2s. His progress up the hill was peculiar. To Ormside, on the same schedule as Nicholson, he dropped four minutes, but he must have won back some time on the earlier stages of the 1 in 100, for the further loss to Mallerstang was only a minute. By that time the poor coal was beginning to tell, and No. 446 was labouring. Where she should have been doing 30 m.p.h. or more she was only making 20 to 25.

At this point Caudle decided to go round the engine with his oil can. It was a routine with drivers to touch up the axle-boxes at least once between Carlisle and Leeds, and this steep pitch was a favourite spot, because the engine was moving more slowly, while the short Birkett Tunnel offered brief protection from the wind. (As so often in the High Pennines it was a gusty night, but rainless.) Modern wick-type lubricators had rendered the trip quite unnecessary, but the established ritual had to be observed. Here I think Caudle showed the limitations of the traditionalist. With a strange fireman, bad coal and an engine losing speed, he should surely have known better than to leave the footplate. No doubt he expected to get back quickly, but the force of the wind delayed him, and by the time he returned they had run past the Mallerstang distant, and neither he nor Follows had seen it. It was of course standing at danger,[1] since the Glasgow train had not been cleared back.

Caudle returned to find his fireman in trouble with the injector—a likely enough happening on a strange engine with this temperamental piece of mechanism. Caudle set himself to put the matter to rights, and not too soon, for the water was near the bottom of the

---

[1] I have used the term 'danger' for distant signals at night while they still showed a red light. This is the term used in the official reports. After the colour was changed to yellow in the 1930s the term changes to 'caution', which is used for daylight throughout. I have followed suit.

glass. He was busy with this just when he was passing the other Mallerstang signals. He did just glimpse the home signal at green, but that was the only one he saw, and it turned out, as we shall see, to be a false indication of safety. It may seem an extraordinary lapse on the part of so experienced a driver, but from what he told the Coroner at the inquest (though he did not mention this at the official inquiry) we can follow his train of thought. An injector out of action, with the engine working hard, would quickly have meant a 'hot boiler', regarded as a serious offence which might render a driver liable to dismissal. So also would running past the signals, if it came to light, but this seemed to Caudle much the lesser risk. He had seen the home signal at green and assumed that the starter would be showing green too. The Glasgow train had left Carlisle nearly a quarter of an hour ahead, so he had no cause to suppose he would be checked at Mallerstang; the contingency of a stalled train obviously did not cross his mind. So he carried on attending to the injector. 'I made the wrong choice,' he said.

Let us now join a rather mystified Signalman Sutherland in Mallerstang box. Having had no clearance for the Glasgow train from Ais Gill he phoned his mate Clemnet there to ask where it was. But Clemnet, with the train out of his view, could only reply that he had no idea. Sutherland therefore kept his signals at danger when he was offered the Edinburgh train from Kirkby Stephen. He observed it travelling rather more slowly than usual, which caused him to think that it was obeying the distant and slowing down. He therefore lowered his home signal with the object of drawing it up to the starter. For this action he was severely criticized by the Inspector, but it should be said in fairness that he was misled by the low speed of the train, and surely a signalman is entitled to assume that a driver will observe all his signals.

But as we have seen, Caudle had missed the distant. As the express approached his box Sutherland realized to his horror that it was still steaming hard. He hurriedly returned his home signal to danger and waved a hand lamp frantically out of the window. But Caudle, preoccupied with his injector, continued pounding his way up the hill.

There was one apparatus Sutherland might have had which would almost certainly have prevented the collision. This was a detonator-placing lever, such as was used by many Companies. By this means a signalman can place a detonator on the rails without leaving his box.

But just as with the lever collar, the Midland would have none of it, a strange attitude for so progressive a railway.

We rejoin Caudle in the cab of No. 446. Not seriously worried about the missed signals, and blissfully unaware of the obstruction ahead, he was keeping a watchful eye on his new fireman's performance with the shovel. He would have done better to keep it on the road. Then his fireman called out: 'Look out, Sam, there's a red light ahead.' It was the tail lamp of the Glasgow train, which Caudle however mistook for the Ais Gill distant, so he whistled for it to come off. He was barely 200 yards from the other train before he realized it was there.

Driver Nicholson of No. 993 had been standing for seven minutes. Looking back he saw a glow in the blackness; it was the red-hot smokebox of No. 446 as she was being thrashed up to the summit. Nicholson at once sent his fireman running back, and Guard Whitley also belatedly started. Nicholson himself whistled and opened his regulator, but still his train would not move. No. 446, steaming almost up to the last moment, crashed into its rear, driving it forward about 15 yards.

Let us ask now, as we did at Hawes Junction: could the collision have been avoided or reduced in violence? In this case there seems no doubt that it could. It is true that Caudle—through his own fault—had only about 200 yards' warning, but a train travelling at 20 m.p.h. up a gradient of 1 in 100 can be pulled up in a much shorter distance than that. Yet the collision was a violent one, showing that No. 446 must have been steaming, as I have said, practically up to the moment of impact. Once again we are forced to conclude that it was a case of a driver who was slow to react.

No. 446 smashed clean through the rear van of the Glasgow train and buried itself in the third-class coach next ahead. The roof of the van shot over the engine and broke open the front compartments of the Edinburgh train, in which a number of passengers were injured, though all the deaths were in the Glasgow train. The engine was smothered in wreckage, so completely that one of the rescuers did not realize it was there until the fire had burned the woodwork away. For just as at Hawes Junction, fire broke out almost at once. There was some doubt about its origin, but Col. Pringle—as he had now become—concluded that it was caused by the escape of gas from cylinders under two of the wrecked vehicles. Since Hawes Junction the Midland had followed the Inspector's easier alternative and had begun to fit its stock with protective valves, but the coaches involved were not so fitted. However extinguishers were brought into use and for fifteen minutes or so the fire appeared to be quelled. Then it broke out again, caused probably by the contents of the ashpan igniting the splintered woodwork round the engine. With the extinguishers exhausted it took a firm hold, and the three rear vehicles of the Glasgow train were burnt out. There was water to be had in plenty, had those on the spot only known. The Glasgow train was standing directly above one of the becks that gush out from the flanks of Wild Boar Fell, but in the darkness no one noticed.

No. 446, the debris burnt off her, stood on the rails, not greatly damaged but with her red paint scorched white by the heat.

Gas was not held responsible for causing or aggravating the second fire. All the same, as the Inspector wrote: 'The case for gas as a standard illuminant is not bettered by the circumstances of this accident.' The Company's vigorous special pleading in defence of gas at the inquiry went to show that it thought so too.

The inquiry was opened at Kirkby Stephen. Since there were Court proceedings likely against Caudle, as we shall see, the Inspector commenced it in private, just as he had done in Gourlay's case at Elliot Junction. But such was the state of public feeling that he agreed to waive the rule, though he moved the sittings to Leeds and later to London. At the outset a contretemps arose, and here we encounter for the first time a new factor in railway affairs: the Trades Unions. The history of the railways' labour relations is no part of our subject, but occasional glimpses have shown that the rule of the managements could be a harsh one. We have seen how Signalman Boote at Hall Road acted hastily through fear of being fined, and in the present case how Driver Caudle made a wrong decision through fear of dismissal. But the railway strike of 1911 had greatly strengthened the Unions' position. Mr. J. H. Thomas, the ex-Great Western goods guard who finished his career as Colonial Secretary in the Baldwin Government, and who was at this time Financial Secretary to the N.U.R., claimed the right to represent the railwaymen concerned. He had obtained information, he said, from some of the men which he intended to put before the inquiry. (Presumably this referred to the coal.) The claim was opposed by the Company's General Superintendent, Mr Cecil Paget, who said he had consulted the drivers, firemen and guards of both trains, and they had decided unanimously that they would not have Mr Thomas to represent them, but wished himself to do so. Intimidation of the worst sort, said Mr Thomas. There had been no suggestion of intimidation, replied Paget. We have decided, as fellow-servants of the same Company, to work together so as best to lay our case before the Government Inspector.

Since Paget was also the son of the Company's Chairman, the words 'fellow-servants' must have sounded odd to the humble railwaymen involved. However he got his way. The Unions were not yet strong enough to force an entry.

At the inquiry the Midland's General Manager, Sir Guy Granet, was at pains to justify the Company's decision to continue building gas-lit carriages. He gave as the reasons: (1) the small number of fires after collisions provably caused by gas, (2) the adoption since these cases of various protective appliances, and (3) 'gas is a better light, and has considerable railway advantages'—meaning that it was more convenient and cheaper.

But Sir Guy was fighting a rearguard action, and the Midland yielded to the pressure. After Ais Gill no more gas-lit carriages were built, though this was not made public until fifteen years later, after the Charfield disaster. The Company also embarked on a modest programme of conversion.

The main inquest on the victims was held at Kirkby Stephen. The jury's first verdict held Driver Caudle, Fireman Follows, Guard Whitley and the Locomotive Superintendent at Carlisle all guilty of negligence—the last-named for failing to provide a pilot. The Coroner refused to accept this, and the jury retired four times in all before they reached an acceptable verdict: Death caused accidentally and by misadventure. They had made it plain that they were not prepared to put anyone in the dock, meaning in particular Driver Caudle. It looked as if he were in the clear.

Alas for Caudle. One passenger, Sir Arthur Percy Douglas, had died in hospital at Carlisle, and the Deputy Coroner there left the jury in no doubt as to what sort of verdict he expected. It was for them to consider, he said:

'whether it was not their duty to return a verdict of manslaughter against one or more of the Company's servants implicated, and particularly against Driver Caudle.'

The jury duly complied, and Caudle was arrested and released on bail of £50.

Caudle stood his trial at the Cumberland Assizes before Mr Justice

Avory, a judge notorious for his harshness. His summing-up was un-
sympathetic, and the jury returned a verdict of guilty, with a strong
recommendation to mercy. Before passing sentence the judge delivered himself of the following *obiter dicta*:

'I have to bear in mind that I sit here not so much for the purpose
of punishing a particular offender as for the purpose of deterring
others from offending in a like manner'—as if any driver needed to
be deterred from putting his own life in danger.

The sentence however was lenient enough: two months in the
second division.

The verdict and sentence caused intense indignation among railwaymen, and there was talk of a strike. But the Midland management, its conscience pricked perhaps by the thought of its own part
in the affair, did the handsome thing. It agreed to pay Caudle's wages
while he was in gaol and to reinstate him thereafter. In fact he was
released almost at once.

Just as Hawes Junction had highlighted a gap in safeguards against
a signalman's failures, so this accident did likewise with regard to
those of drivers. I have said in the foreword that at the beginning of
the century there were no safeguards against a driver's failure to
observe the signals, and no progress had been made since, except on
one line. This was the Great Western, which in 1906 had started
experimenting with a system of audible cab warning, applied at the
distant signal, and was at this time in process of installing on its
main lines. I have explained in the last chapter how the system works
in present-day conditions; if it had been in operation at Mallerstang
it would certainly have caused Caudle to bring his train to a stop.
Col. Pringle in his report drew attention to this, as he and his fellow-
inspectors were to do time and again thereafter. But many, many
years were to pass; the old Companies were to be merged into the
grouped systems and the groups swallowed up in British Railways,
before at long last the decision was taken to apply the system to all
main lines, a process which even now is by no means complete.

CHAPTER 9

QUINTINSHILL
CALEDONIAN RAILWAY

Of the three Scottish accidents recorded in this book, two occurred in December snowstorms. The third took place in the brilliant sunshine of a spring morning. Of all places Gretna, scene of romance, became the scene of the greatest slaughter in the history of Britain's railways.

Saturday, May 22, 1915, dawned fine and clear on the Border, giving the promise of a glorious day. The war had been in progress for nine months, but it had brought no change to the life of Signalman James Tinsley, except to make him busier in his box at Quintinshill, about a mile and a half to the north of Gretna station. This morning he was on the 6 a.m. shift, which meant getting up earlier than suited either him or his mate George Meakin, who shared the duties turn and turn about. So the two had worked out a scheme to give each other an extra half-hour in bed. After six o'clock the night shift man would write the train register entries on slips of paper, which the day man could copy into the book when he arrived about 6.30. The arrangement was of course quite unauthorized, but it had worked successfully for a couple of years. For Tinsley, who lived in the railway cottages by Gretna station, it was especially handy on those days when the 6.10 slow from Carlisle was shunted onto the loop at Quintinshill (where there was no station) to let a couple of night expresses from Euston pass. These were due out of Carlisle at 5.50 and 6.5, and if they were late the local was sent on ahead, as it had a connection to make at Beattock. When this happened the signalman at Quintinshill would send a message that 'the boy would get a ride today', which the Gretna man passed on to Tinsley.

So it was on this morning. Tinsley duly mounted the footplate of the local at Gretna, creeping round the back of the train in case the stationmaster should be early astir. At Quintinshill traffic was building up. The down loop was already occupied by the 4.50 a.m. goods from Carlisle, which was likewise waiting for the expresses to pass, while waiting to enter the up loop was a returning 'Jellicoe Special', one of the trains which carried coal from the Welsh pits to the Grand Fleet at Scapa Flow, and for which there was no room in the sidings at Carlisle. So there was nothing for it but to put the local train across on to the up line; this had happened on the average about once a month.

Tinsley jumped off the engine—No. 907, of the 'Cardean' class— as it was being shunted through the crossover. He found quite a party in the box, for in addition to Meakin there were three trainmen from the waiting goods trains. Tinsley immediately applied himself to the register, in which there were fifteen entries to be made—five each in respect of the three trains which had passed since six o'clock.

Meakin meanwhile accepted the empty coal train on to the up loop, and clearance was given to Kirkpatrick box to the north, though whether by him or Tinsley was never established. At all events the Kirkpatrick man was now free, as he supposed, to offer another train. The first express, which had left Carlisle at 6.27, was accepted and ran past.

What Meakin failed to do was to protect the local. A train standing on its wrong line can obviously become a source of danger, and a series of safeguards have been devised to prevent the possibility of a collision. In the Caledonian's case the first safety device consisted of the lever collar, but Meakin did not place one on the up home signal lever. This was not just a lapse of the moment; he told the inquiry that the collar was hardly ever used in the box. Before condemning him let us recall that the Companies themselves were not agreed on whether the collar was necessary or even desirable. More serious was Meakin's omission to take the second protective step, namely, to send the Blocking Back Within Home Signal code and set his train indicator at Train On Line, which would have prevented Kirkpatrick from even offering another train. There was company in the box, and the war news to discuss from the morning paper which Tinsley had brought; we must suppose that these distractions caused him to forget.

Enter another neglectful party. Fireman Hutchinson of the local came into the box to remind the signalman and sign the train book, as required by Rule 55. But under the Rule he should have made sure, before leaving the box, that his train was properly protected, and this he omitted to do. 'My train was right outside the box,' he said later. 'Tinsley could see it there.' Which was true enough, if Tinsley had been looking. But that individual was still busy with his writing. He also probably had his back to the window; so at least is suggested by the layout of the box, which is unusual in having its frame at the rear.

At 3.42 that morning the first of two troop trains had left Larbert for Liverpool. They were conveying the 1/7 Royal Scots, a Territorial battalion drawn from Leith and Musselburgh, to embark on the troopship *Empress of Britain* en route for the Dardanelles. The battalion had been earmarked for France, but the ill-fated Gallipoli campaign was going badly, and so it was being diverted there. This first train consisted of A and D Companies, together with the C.O. and the headquarters staff—498 officers and men. Troop trains are not noted for their luxury appointments; this one consisted of fifteen vehicles borrowed from the Great Central Railway, mostly old six-wheelers with wooden frames, in which the men were travelling, with all their kit, eight to a compartment. Six Caledonian vans were attached at the rear for the baggage. The driver, Scott, a Carlisle man, was something of an aristocrat among drivers, for he had driven three generations of Royalty—Victoria, Edward VII and George V. He was in charge of McIntosh superheated 4-4-0 No. 121 as he and his fireman set out upon their last journey.

It was 6.43 at Quintinshill. Meakin, off duty now, was sitting reading out the war news to the company in the box. From Kirkpatrick came the bell signal offering the troop train. Tinsley, preoccupied with his writing, had forgotten all about the standing local, and he had nothing to remind him. Accepted, he rang back. At 6.47 he obtained acceptance from Gretna and pulled off his signals. About the same time he accepted the second express, and cleared his signals for that also.

Now here is a remarkable fact. On the spot were six enginemen trained in the art of reading signals, as well as three guards and two signalmen; eleven railwaymen in all. Yet not one of them noticed that the signals had been cleared for the troop train while the local was standing in its path.

Driver Scott was travelling fast down the 1 in 200 gradient. The obstructing local first came into view when he was 280 yards away—nothing like distance enough in which to bring his train to a stop. What attempt he made to do so will never be known, but the train was still moving at a high speed when it struck the local. Contemporary accounts, based on survivors' stories, suggest that the effects of this first collision were relatively slight, but this can hardly have been the case. No. 907 was driven back 40 yards and came to rest on the 'six-foot' with her tender across the down line. The engine of the troop train was flung on its side across both running lines. The foremost of the Great Central carriages shot clean over its engine and landed some distance in front of it, and the remaining carriages were spreadeagled over both tracks. A 213-yard train was compressed into 67 yards. It was a major catastrophe in its own right.

Meakin was going down the steps of the box when the collision sent him running back. 'Whatever have you done, Jimmy?' he cried out. 'Good heavens,' exclaimed Tinsley, 'whatever can be wrong?' 'You've got the Parly[1] standing there,' said Meakin, and a sudden horrifying thought struck him. 'Where's the 6.5?' he cried out, and rushed to put the down signals to danger. The same thought also struck Guard Graham of the local, who had quickly picked himself up from the floor of his van, as well as to the driver and fireman of the coal empties train. All three started to race up the line waving their arms, Graham in the lead. Too late. Graham had covered 167 yards in 31 seconds—not bad for a middle-aged man—when the express was upon them. At its head were 4-4-os Nos. 48 and 140, the latter as pilot to Beattock summit, and the engines had worked up to a good sixty on the gently falling track out of Carlisle. Both drivers saw the gesticulating figures; they shut off steam and applied the brakes. But they could do little more than check speed before ploughing into the wreckage, and into the soldiers who were escaping after the first collision. Just 53 seconds had elapsed between the two collisions.

The leading engine struck the tender of the troop train engine and drove it for 30 yards through the wagons of the goods train on the down loop. Its own tender mounted the framing of the train engine, and the first three coaches were telescoped. On top of the heaped-up engines was piled a vast mountain of debris, which caught fire almost at once. All the Great Central coaches were gas-lit, and their cylinders had been re-charged just before leaving Larbert. Coals from the troop train engine ignited the escaping gas, and soon the whole train was ablaze. Extinguishers, the water in the good engines' tenders, water pumped from a local stream and the Carlisle fire brigade—all were powerless to check it. All that day and throughout the next night the pyramid of wreckage blazed, consuming the dead and the living alike.

---

[1] i.e. 'Parliamentary'. Expression for a slow train. Originally used for a train at the statutory fare of 1d a mile.

Eye-witnesses were to describe the scene: the flames, not lurid as at night but angry and red; the billowing smoke grey-yellow in the bright sunshine, the hissing of the engines, the pop-popping of the ammunition from the officers' pistols, and—a touch from the local reporter:

'The strangely incongruous mingling of human cries of anguish with the sweet trills of the mavis and the blackbird as they poured forth their morning song from the neighbouring trees.'

The lucky ones were killed outright. Scores of others had to wait helplessly for the fire to reach them. Men burning to death begged their rescuers to shoot them.

The entire troop train was destroyed, save only the vans at the rear. These had broken away on the recoil of the first collision, and despite the gradient had run some distance up the line, where the brakeman of the empty coal train managed to secure them. The first three coaches of the express were burnt out, as well as seven wagons of the down goods and five of the empty coal train. Thus Quintinshill achieved another record: that of involving five trains. The fire burned for over twenty-four hours, and all the coal in the engines' tenders was consumed. The last bodies were brought out on the Sunday afternoon, but more portions of bodies were recovered later.

In this disaster 226 people perished—more than in any other two British railway accidents put together. Of these 214[1] were in the troop train, seven in the express, two in the local (which was nearly empty), while three were railwaymen. The third, besides Driver Scott and his fireman, was a sleeping-car attendant in the express. Both crews of the express escaped miraculously with bruises; the driver and fireman of the local took refuge under the empty coal train as the troop train bore down upon them.

Few of the survivors among the troops escaped injury. When the remnant was paraded at 4 p.m. only fifty-four were there to give their names. The two companies in the second train were sent on to the Dardanelles, where they quickly suffered heavy casualties.

Of the engines concerned, No. 121 of the troop train was damaged

---

[1] The number of killed given in the official report is 227, including 215 troops, but the number 214 is quoted by the C.O., Lt. Col. W. Carmichael Peebles, in his history of the battalion, and is confirmed by the names on the memorial in the Rosebank Cemetery at Leith. The battalion rolls were lost in the accident, which caused a good deal of confusion. It was stated at the subsequent trial that some men who had been believed killed had turned up at the Dardanelles.

beyond repair. No. 907, one of only seven heavy 4-6-0s owned by the Caledonian, was scrapped after an attempt had been made to repair her.

Most of the injured were taken to hospital in Carlisle. Some died on the way, others after arrival. Since they had died in England an inquest had to be held, and the jury returned a verdict of manslaughter against Tinsley, Meakin and the fireman Hutchinson. This raised a curious legal point. The Coroner said he had no choice but to commit the men to the Cumberland Assizes, although their lawyer argued that he had no power to do so, since the alleged offence had been committed in Scotland. But the men had already been charged by the Dumfriesshire police, and thus made legal history by being indicted for the same offence in both the English and the Scottish courts.

All three stood their trial in Edinburgh in the following September on the charge that: By breaches of duty they caused the collision and thus did kill Frank Scott (the driver) and about half-a-dozen other named persons. The case against Hutchinson did not stand up, and he was discharged. The two signalmen presented pitiful figures in the dock. They had suffered, said their Counsel, in shocking fashion. Both had had nervous breakdowns, and they had suffered from sleeplessness and mental anguish. Surely forgetfulness, pleaded Counsel, is not a criminal offence, however tragic its consequences. But the negligence had been too glaring, and the results too terrible. Scottish juries do not have to be unanimous but this one was, and it was out for only eight minutes before returning a verdict of guilty. Tinsley, who was held to bear the greater blame, was sentenced to three years' imprisonment, and Meakin to eighteen months. In due course mercy prevailed, and both men were released after they had served a year. They had already been sentenced to the greater punishment of a lifetime's remorse.

Quintinshill box is still there, just across the fields from Gretna. The loops are there, though looking a trifle rusty these days. The up line is now track-circuited, but the down line offers no more protection than then against a similar chain of human failures. Nothing much else is changed from that spring morning when more than two hundred men of the Royal Scots met death on their own soil, before more hundreds of their comrades met death of a different kind at the Dardanelles.

CHAPTER 10

WEEDON

LONDON & NORTH WESTERN RAILWAY

For the third time in eight years the London & North Western figures in an accident: a sad record for such a well-managed system. In its day the self-styled Premier Line was a very splendid railway. It laid claim to the finest permanent way in the world, and it was not an empty boast, though the Great Western and Great Northern might have challenged it. In the care of its locomotives it probably came second only to the Great Western. The clank of loose coupling-rods, sure sign of a badly-maintained engine, was seldom heard on the North Western.

It was the greater irony therefore that the Weedon disaster on August 14, 1915, should be caused through a fault in maintenance. It was a fault of the most trivial kind, yet it wrecked a train and caused the deaths of ten people. After the vast calamity of Quintinshill three months earlier it attracted but little notice; I include it here because among major accidents it is unique. It is the only case where a defect in one train caused the wreck of another.

Driver Brightland, in charge of George the Fifth Class 4-4-0 No. 1489 'Wolfhound', was at the head of the 8.45 a.m. semi-fast from Birmingham New Street to Euston. While the train was standing at Rugby he left the footplate to oil his engine, and noticed that the split pin on the right hand driving wheel was missing. This pin held in place the screw washer retaining the coupling rod on its crankpin. We encounter here a mystery to which the records provide no answer: how and when had the pin dropped out? It must have been in place when 'Wolfhound' left Monument Lane sheds to run down to New Street, and somewhere in the 30 miles between there and Rugby it had come adrift. As we shall see in a minute, we are left asking how it was that the events at Weedon had not already taken place before

Rugby. For though the pin was missing, the washer was still fully screwed on its thread.

Brightland reported the loss to the Bank engineman at Rugby, Hammond, and asked for a replacement. It so happened that one of the fitters at Rugby shed, Oldham, was on the platform seeing off some relations by this train. Hammond asked Oldham if he could fit another pin. Being on the platform already, and rather than hold up the train by going for a new pin to the stores, Oldham said that he would get one from another engine, No. 665, which was shunting in the yard nearby. We are left wondering how No. 665 could safely carry on without this small but vital part; presumably it belonged to Rugby shed and the pin could be replaced at leisure.

Oldham went over to No. 665, borrowed a hammer and knocked out the pin, which he brought over and drove in, as he supposed, tight. To keep a split pin in position it is necessary to open the ends, for which purpose a chisel was generally used. Oldham had no chisel, but used the jaws of a 5/8" spanner, or so he said. The whole operation, including fetching the pin, had taken only five minutes, and Brightland's train left on time.

'Wolfhound' had just passed through Weedon, 13 miles south of Rugby, when Brightland heard his fireman shout 'Whoa'. The fireman had applied the brake, and Brightland closed the regulator. The engine gave a lurch. Brightland looked out on his own side—the left—and could see nothing wrong. Then he crossed over to the fireman's side, and there saw the ballast flying. Quickly he opened his sand valves and brought the train to a standstill an engine's length inside Stowe Hill tunnel.

It was then discovered what had happened. The split pin had fallen out and the screw washer had unthreaded itself and dropped off. It was found later between the platforms in Weedon station. Without the washer to hold it, the coupling-rod had come off the crank-pin. As it flailed around loose it struck a sleeper on the down road and displaced the track. It had then bent over double and was forced back with its leading end against the tender steps. If it had bent inwards it would have derailed its own engine; as it was, it derailed a train on the other line. No passengers were injured in the Birmingham train, though all the right-hand carriage windows were broken by the flying ballast.

Just about as Brightland was closing his regulator the second portion of the day Irish Mail passed on the down line, double-headed by

Precedent class 1189 'Stewart'—of the same class as 'Cook' which had come to grief at Ditton Junction—and Renown class 4-4-0 No. 1971 'Euryalus', one of the Webb 4-cylinder compounds rebuilt by Whale as simples. They were hauling a 15-coach load and were travelling at about 70 m.p.h. as they came out of Stowe Hill tunnel. Driver Hadfield of 'Stewart' had just time to notice ballast being thrown up into his cab when the engine struck the displaced section and was derailed, with the train engine behind it. Neither engine was overturned, but the coaches scattered in all directions. Half-a-dozen or so were spreadeagled across both lines; others fell down on to the right hand side of the embankment, while the postal sorting vans fell to the left. Two postal sorters were among those killed. Only the dining saloons and the four rear coaches remained on the track. A dire consequence indeed of the loss of a minute object, and belonging to another train at that. It was only fortunate that 'Wolfhound' stopped where it did. A few yards further and the derailment would have taken place inside the tunnel, with consequences to both trains that do not bear thinking of.

There could be no doubt about it: the hasty job of work at Rugby had caused the disaster. 'I cannot help thinking,' wrote the Inspecting Officer, Lt. Col. Druitt, 'that Oldham in his desire not to delay the train did not open the split pin as he described, but merely bent it slightly when hitting it on its split end, and so loosened it.' It would have been better, thought the Inspector, if he had obtained a new pin from the stores. The Inspector also suggested that the washers in question should in future have left-handed and right-handed threads, so that even if their pins were lost they would not unscrew themselves in this way.

But we are still left with the riddle: how did 'Wolfhound' manage to travel an unknown distance before Rugby minus the pin without the washer unthreading itself by so much as a single turn, when within the next 15 miles—even if the new pin had fallen out straight-away—it had unthreaded itself completely? To that question it seems there is no answer.

Thirty-six years later another accident occurred less than half a mile away, at the south end of Stowe Hill Tunnel. This was on September 21, 1951, when the bogie wheels of Stanier Pacific No. 46207, 'Princess Arthur of Connaught', hauling the 8.20 from Liverpool to Euston, left the rails, causing the engine to plunge down the embankment followed by eight of its fifteen coaches. As in the case of the earlier accident, it was a mercy that the derailment did not take place inside the tunnel. In terms of lives lost this second accident was more serious than the first; fifteen people were killed. So Weedon joins the ill-starred list of places—Norton Fitzwarren and Winsford are two others, as we shall see—which have twice been the scene of a major disaster.

CHAPTER 11

ABERMULE
CAMBRIAN RAILWAYS

In the heyday of the silent films one of the favourite themes was a railway collision. The two trains would come rushing towards each other on the single track, and then (by means of models) we saw them collide. It all seemed very American; not at all the sort of thing that could happen here. It did happen here, twice back in the 1870s at Norwich on the Great Eastern and at Radstock on that unspeakably bad railway (as it then was) the Somerset & Dorset, in both cases at night, and once in broad daylight at Abermule on the Cambrian Railways on January 16, 1921.

Here for the only time in this book we encounter one of the minor pre-grouping lines. The Cambrian traversed those parts of Wales into which none of the greater Companies had found it worth while to extend. Its main line ran from Whitchurch in Shropshire to Aberystwyth, and it wandered over the country's desolate interior from Brecon in the south to Pwllheli in the north. Where industry and population abounded, there the Cambrian was not. Save for an outlying branch to Wrexham, it served not a single town with as many as 20,000 inhabitants. It was in short a poor and not very efficient railway, until the Great Western took it over at the grouping and gave it a face-lift. What I have called the easy Welsh informality may or may not have characterized its operations as a whole; that quality was certainly very much in evidence at Abermule.

The now-closed station at Abermule, lying between the ancient borough of Montgomery and the present-day county town of Newtown, was just a little more than a wayside station, for it was the junction for a short branch line to the market town of Kerry. Like the whole of the Cambrian, the line was single, with passing places at most of the stations. It was worked under the system invented by Edward Tyer, who must certainly have imagined that he had evolved a foolproof method of preventing collisions on a single line. Its essence is that its operation requires action by the signalman at both ends of a single-line section. The tablets giving the train authority to proceed are locked in an instrument, and a tablet can only be withdrawn if the man in charge of the instrument at the other end presses a plunger. When a tablet has been taken out an electrical circuit is broken, and a second tablet cannot be withdrawn from either instrument until the first tablet has been replaced in the instrument at the other end, or has been returned to its original instrument.

You would have thought that such a system could not possibly go wrong. But Tyer had reckoned without the gang of incompetents at Abermule.

This quartet consisted of a signalman, Jones, and two youngsters, the porter Rogers aged 17 and an odd-job lad of 15 called Thompson, together with the man in charge, relief Stationmaster Lewis, doing duty for the regular man Parry who was on holiday. Of the four we have the clearest picture of Thompson, a simple lad, willing but dim; in the words of the Coroner, the sort of lad who was ready to oblige the stationmaster or signalman if they felt disinclined to move about. Now it will be obvious that the Tyer system demands that the man at either end shall know exactly what the other is doing, and it is therefore strictly laid down that only authorized persons shall work the tablet instruments. The authorized persons in this case were the stationmaster and the signalman, but a go-as-you-please system had grown up whereby anyone did the job who happened to be at hand. For this the regular stationmaster Parry was responsible, but his stand-in Lewis had accepted these casual methods without question: doubtless they were not confined to Abermule. Here however there was a special circumstance. The tablet instruments, instead of being in the signal box, were in a room by the booking hall on the opposite platform. It saved Jones' legs therefore to send one of the boys to withdraw or replace a tablet, in which case they would also sign the train book, likewise strictly against the rules.

Thus it had gone on for a long time. In the twenty years and more since the Tyer system had been installed on the line there had never been an accident, and nobody contemplated the possibility of one. Until this day.

Two trains were due to cross at Abermule about mid-day: a down (westbound) slow and an up train that might by courtesy be called an express and was booked non-stop from Newtown to Welshpool. Though Abermule was the normal crossing point, this might take place at either Montgomery or Newtown if one or the other train happened to be late. On this day the relief stationmaster Lewis was away at dinner, while Rogers and Thompson were having theirs in the booking office. Jones was in the instrument room nearby. At 11.52 the slow was belled from Montgomery; Jones accepted it and plunged on the instrument to enable his colleague there to release the tablet. Jones entered Train Entering Section at 11.55. He then phoned Moat Lane Junction, the station on the far side of Newtown, to inquire about the whereabouts of the express. He was told that it had just gone by. He then left for the signalbox, having told Rogers that the slow had left Montgomery three or four minutes before and that the express had passed Moat Lane, thus making it clear that he was expecting them to pass at Abermule. He then opened the level crossing gates and pulled off the down home signal.

At this point Lewis returned from his lunch, but neither Jones nor Roberts told him that the express was between Moat Lane and Newtown. His habit was to be on the platform when the trains crossed, but on this occasion he found waiting for him Permanent Way Inspector Thomas, who wanted a wagon for loading some stake wood. Thomas was in a hurry, for he wanted to be away by the slow train, so Lewis went down with him to the goods yard.

Meanwhile at 11.56 the express had been belled from Newtown. With no one else about Rogers went to the instrument room, acknowledged the bell signal and plunged on the Newtown-Abermule instrument to release the tablet at Newtown for the express. He had done this many times before, and it did not occur to him to tell anyone. He then went off to the ground frame at the west end of the platform to set the road for the express.

At 11.59 Train Entering Section was belled from Newtown. Lewis was in the goods yard, Jones was in the signal box, Rogers was at the ground frame; where Thompson was is not related. At all events there was no one to acknowledge Newtown's signal, which was not entered in the train book.

At 12.2, when the slow train arrived, Thompson was there, and since no one else was about he collected the tablet from the engine crew. At this point Lewis came hurrying up from the goods yard, having heard the train arrive. Thompson handed him the tablet with the words: 'Change this tablet, Frank, I am going to collect the tickets.' That at least is what he intended to convey, but he had an impediment in his speech and Lewis thought he had said: 'Take

74

this tablet, the train is going on.' So Lewis assumed that Thompson had already changed the tablet under orders from Jones. Lewis asked where the express was, and the halfwit Thompson replied: 'About Moat Lane'—presumably because he had heard Jones say so some minutes earlier. With that the lad went off to collect the ticket from the solitary passenger who had alighted. Lewis assumed the express was late, and told Thompson, who had now returned, to go and tell Jones to pull off for the slow train. It was all very haphazard, but since the train crew had not yet been given the tablet it was not necessarily fatal. The next piece of carelessness was. All tablets are marked with the sections to which they refer, and it did not occur to Lewis to look and see if he was handing over the right tablet. Nor did the fireman think to examine it; he took it without removing it from its pouch. With that Lewis gave the right away.

Meanwhile Rogers could not understand why he could not move the ground frame levers. They were locked from the signal box, and naturally could not be moved for the up loop line while the down starting signal was off. But Rogers does not appear to have noticed this signal. After some hesitation he was about to shout to Jones to release the signal box lever when he saw Lewis give the down train the right away. If the stationmaster gave it, he thought, it must be in order, and he assumed that the express must have been held up at Newtown.

Let us review the catalogue of wrong assumptions. Thompson assumed that Lewis knew the tablets had not been changed. Lewis assumed that Thompson had changed them. Jones assumed that the express had not been accepted from Newtown, and Rogers assumed that it had been held there. The engine crew assumed that they had been handed the right tablet. With a light-hearted disregard of all the rules two trains had been set on a collision course from which nothing could save them.

After the train had left Thompson went into the instrument room to bell Train Entering Section to Newtown. He looked at the instruments. The Montgomery-Abermule instrument had not been cleared, while the Abermule-Newtown one showed that a tablet had been withdrawn for the express. He called Lewis, who rang Newtown in haste. 'Has the express left yet?' he asked. 'It left at 11.59,' came the reply. In a despairing attempt Lewis 'waved' the up distant signal, i.e. put it quickly up and down, in the hope of attracting the slow driver's attention, but probably the train was already past the signal.

The collision took place about a mile from Abermule. When the crew of the slow train saw the express, if at all, will never be known, for both were killed. But they could not have been keeping a good lookout, for their engine was steaming up to the moment it struck the express.

Driver Jones and Fireman Owen of the express, on the other hand, were fully alert. Jones comes across to us as a conscientious type. He had accepted the tablet in person at Newtown—that was generally considered the fireman's job—and had examined it before leaving. Now he was not relaxing his lookout between signals as some drivers are apt to do. Running downhill at about 50 m.p.h. he first saw the slow train some 300 yards away, belching exhaust as it laboured up the bank at 30 m.p.h. or so. He did what he could in the few seconds available. He shut off steam and applied the brake, slowing his train appreciably as the other came heedlessly on. When it was about two engines' lengths away he and his fireman jumped.

Now it was possible to observe what a head-one crash was really like. The locomotives—both 4-4-0s—were fantastically twisted. The boiler of the express engine was wrenched from its frame and thrown beside the track facing in the opposite direction. The engine of the slow train reared straight on end like a bucking horse. In the space of 50 yards both engines and five coaches—four from the express and one from the slow—normally occupying 110 yards, formed a tangled mass of wreckage. The express suffered the worst, and most of the fifteen passengers killed were in its second and third coaches. Among them was Lord Herbert Vane-Tempest, a Director of the Cambrian. Luckiest were the occupants of the express's first coach, which was torn from its bogies and landed upright athwart them; no one in it was seriously injured. Nine of the thirteen coaches were gas-lit, but there was no fire. For some reason eight of them—four in each train—belonged to the London & North Western.

Jones somersaulted three times as he jumped and landed up underneath a carriage. His neck was badly cut but he was not otherwise seriously injured, and his first thought was to retrieve the tablets. He called out to his fireman, who although also hurt began to search among the wreckage and eventually found both—his own and the Montgomery-Abermule one, telling its own fatal tale. 'Oh Tom,' he told his brother as he lay in the infirmary that night. 'I am so glad there is no blame attached to me. It was I who took the tablet at Newtown.'

In his report the Inspecting Officer, Col. Pringle, had some scorching criticisms to make of methods at Abermule:

'Such a tale of failure in broad daylight, and of misunderstanding on the part of so many men, would have been incredible prior to the accident. Indiscipline and slipshod methods of custody and transference of tablets on the part of the traffic staff, combined with failure on the part of enginemen to examine tablets, could alone have made this disaster possible.'

The Inspector also criticized the practice of having the tablet instruments installed in the station buildings instead of in the signal box. This represented a change of official viewpoint as a result of the accident. At the inquest the Inspector had told the Coroner that hitherto the Ministry had seen no good reason why the tablets should be kept in the signal box. The other method was usual on the Highland Railway and on the single lines of the London & North Western. However, he added, we live and learn.

At the inquest proceedings there re-appears the figure of J. H. Thomas, now promoted to General Secretary of the N.U.R. and very much the man in command. He subjected both the management representatives and his own members to a grilling cross-examination. From the Superintendent of the Line he drew the admission that neither Rogers nor Thompson had his signature to use the tablet instruments, although no one without it had authority to do so. Lewis's story that Rogers was working the instrument for instructional purposes was quickly demolished. Thomas's questions to Jones the signalman ran thus:

THOMAS: Was there any change in the general method of running the station on this day compared with other days?
JONES: No, sir.
THOMAS: So that the method of Thompson putting entries in that book, Rogers putting entries in that book, Rogers getting hold of a tablet and Thompson getting a tablet, is the system at the station?
JONES: Yes.

It was impossible to hold the two youths responsible. The jury pinned the blame on Lewis and Jones, though it may be thought that the regular stationmaster Parry, who had allowed the lax working to grow up, was lucky to escape. The jury's first verdict was to find Lewis and Jones guilty of gross neglect, but the Coroner reminded them that this was equivalent to a verdict of manslaughter, which had not been their intention. So they retired again and came back with the verdict that the two men were guilty of great neglect calling for very severe censure, which the Coroner proceeded to administer.

Both Lewis and Jones were seen to be in tears as the Coroner addressed them.

CHAPTER 12

HULL PARAGON

LONDON & NORTH EASTERN RAILWAY

We speak of the million-to-one chance, but if there is such a thing as an infinity-to-one-chance, this was it. A signalman had three-tenths of a second in which to make a once-in-a-lifetime mistake, and in that split fraction of time he managed to make it. It happened at the approach to Hull Paragon station on the morning of February 14, 1927.

That February was an unlucky month at Paragon. Only nine days earlier a sidelong collision had taken place between two incoming trains, one from Hornsea and an L.M.S. excursion from Halifax, caused by the L.N.E.R. pilotman on the excursion misreading the signals. Both trains were badly damaged, but total casualties amounted to only three injured.

The collision on February 14th was a much more serious affair. It was one of the rare head-on type, though not of course of the single-line genre that we encountered at Abermule. An outgoing train to Scarborough was diverted on to its wrong line and collided with an incoming train from Withernsea. To explain what happened I must draw a sketch of part of the approaches to the station :

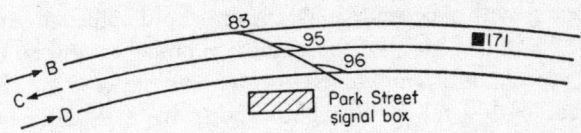

The numbers shown are those of the levers in the Park Street box. No. 171 is the C road signal, i.e. for outgoing trains; the other three numbers are points. I have shown only the numbers with which we are concerned. The crossing was the same one over which the

Hornsea train had been travelling in the earlier accident; the collision with the excursion took place at No. 96 points.

We must now move to West Parade Junction, 480 yards further out. The 8.22 a.m. from Withernsea, in the charge of N.E.R. Class F 4-4-0 No. 96 and filled with office workers and schoolchildren, was approaching the junction at about 15 m.p.h. It was running about nine minutes late. Driver Dixon had already shut off steam for the stop and had his hand ready on the brake handle. Spanning the junction is the Argyle Street road bridge, and as he emerged from underneath it Dixon raised his eyes to look for the West Park starting signal, which was at clear. On dropping his eyes again he was confronted by the spectacle of a train approaching him on the same line a mere couple of engine lengths away. He had only time to apply the brake before the trains collided.

Driver Atkinson was in charge of M Class No. 1628, very similar to Class F, on the 9.5 a.m. Hull to Scarborough. He came out of the station along C road and at the Park Street home gantry received the centre of three signals, No. 171, applicable to a straight movement along the road. He noticed nothing unusual as he went by Park Street box, though he might have done. It was only when he lost sight of the West Park home signal, which ought to have been clear in view, that it seemed to him there was something wrong. A water crane, too, on the right seemed closer than it should have been. Atkinson crossed over to the fireman's side and then back to his own. There could be no doubt about it. Somehow or other he had been put across onto the incoming B road, the road along which the Withernsea train was approaching. At this moment no train was in sight, but Atkinson lost no time in shutting off steam and applying the brake. The next thing he knew was a violent impact, which buried him in a shower of coal from the tender. He had very nearly brought his train to a standstill.

Compared with Abermule it was a very mild collision. At Abermule the combined speed of the trains was probably near 60 m.p.h.; here it was about 15 m.p.h. Neither engine suffered much more than front end damage. But both trains were extensively telescoped, and twelve passengers were killed. Most of the dead were in the Withernsea train; they included two schoolboys.

Most of the coaches in both trains were gas-lit, but there was no fire.

Turning off Argyle Street is Anlaby Road, where stands a workhouse. 'There was a touch of providence,' wrote the *Hull Evening News*, 'in the fact that the accident took place bang at the rear of the workhouse infirmary.' Aid from that quarter was quickly forthcoming. Less helpful was the attitude of some workhouse official. A Mr Leonard Walker had been crossing the Argyle Street bridge at the time and had actually seen the collision. He hurried round to the workhouse to telephone for help, but was told that as the accident had not taken place on workhouse premises he could not use the phone.

Let us see what had been happening in the Park Street box. This was worked by the electro-pneumatic system, which had been installed twenty-one years earlier and which, among other advantages, considerably eases the signalman's labours. It was manned by three signalmen, who took turns three weeks at a time to act as chargeman. In charge on this day was Alfred Campling, who was actually the junior of the three, with his two assistants, Clark and Gibson. Clark was the eldest; he had forty-six years' service, and in him we discern the authentic conservative with a small 'c'. He did not hold with this new-fangled electro-pneumatic apparatus, and half-believed, I think, that it went wrong at times through sheer cussedness. This did not affect his actions, but it certainly affected his attitude afterwards. 'I know that the points do not do as they ought to do,' he told the inquiry.

The Withernsea train was due to be put across from B to D road via points 83 and 96, thus crossing the path of the Scarborough train on C road. 'Right away Scarborough,' called out Campling to his assistants, 'and B to D for Withernsea as soon as the Scarborough is out.' Gibson returned signal 171 behind the Scarborough train, while Clark set the road for the Withernsea train. The operation was performed at speed, for since the Withernsea train was already late the signalmen were anxious not to delay it further. According to the rules, Gibson should have waited to restore 171 lever until the whole train had passed the signal, though in my observation this is a rule which is seldom strictly observed by signalmen. In this case Gibson restored the lever when the engine and the first three coaches, out of five, were past. Whatever the letter of the rule, he was acting with the good of the service in mind. If only he had been able to foresee the result of his couple of seconds' premature action!

As the Scarborough train passed, the signalmen heard a curious clicking noise in the frame, and then, as it was running out of sight,

Gibson said; 'Where has that chap gone?' 'What chap?' asked Clark, to which Gibson replied: 'Well, I thought that Scarborough looked a bit too far over.'

A few minutes later Driver Atkinson came into the box. When he had extricated himself from the coal he had sat down on the ballast for a few minutes to recover, then he set off for the box. 'What are you playing at this morning?' he asked Campling. The latter turned to Clark. 'Did you pull that lever over?' he asked. Clark made no reply. Atkinson saw that the signalmen, as he put it, were a bit flustered, so he said no more and left the box.

How had the Scarborough train got transferred to B road? It could only have been through the No. 95 points. Yet these points were interlocked with signal 171 so that when the signal was at clear the points were locked in the straight position. Moreover they were equipped with facing point locking bars—long bars placed ahead of the points which are depressed by the wheels of a train. This locks the points and prevents any movement just before and during the time when the train is passing over them. Yet in spite of this double precaution No. 95 points had been pulled over. After much careful investigation the Inspecting Officer, Col. Pringle, found the answer. When No. 171 signal was restored, before the train had fully passed, this had freed the interlocking. At that moment, the Inspector calculated, the train was 37.81 feet from the facing point locking bars, when the points would again have become locked. Tests indicated that the train had been travelling at 13.75 m.p.h., so that it would have covered the distance in 1.9 seconds. For that period of time No. 95 points were free. During that time Clark must have moved them in mistake for No. 96, an action which, including the moving of the locking bar lever, was timed to take 1.6 seconds. Three-tenths of a second sooner or later, and disaster would have been averted. Three-tenths of a second for Clark's mistake, possibly the only one of his career, to prove fatal. A one-in-infinity chance if ever there was one. If Gibson, too, had waited for the passage of just one further coach before restoring the lever, the engine would have been on the locking bar and safe.

Now the clicking noise which the signalmen had heard was explained. It was made by lever 83 and its connections as the Scarborough train ran through the trailing points which were set against it.

The Inspector ascribed the accident to the human factor. The

Withernsea train had already been signalled Train Entering Section to Park Street box, and if it had been held up it would have been Gibson's duty to record the fact.

'It is human nature,' wrote the Inspector, 'for men, who take an honest pride in their work, to avoid if possible having to book the stoppage of a train, especially one already late, at a signal for the working of which they are responsible.' Both Gibson and Clark had acted more hurriedly than they should have done.

At the inquiry Clark appeared as a sorely puzzled man. He had been unable to eat or sleep, he said, for trying to think how the Scarborough train had got on the wrong line. He stoutly denied that he had pulled the wrong lever, and instanced various cases of where the electro-pneumatic system had gone wrong. I doubt if he was ever really convinced that it was not the system, but himself, that was to blame.

CHAPTER 13

SEVENOAKS

SOUTHERN RAILWAY

One of the commonest of minor railway mishaps is a derailment. Most of us at one time or another have seen a vehicle off the line. But derailment at speed, caused by defects of rolling stock or track, has been among the rarest causes of accidents in Britain. Where a locomotive has become derailed it has generally been a tank engine, and there have been three notable accidents of this sort during the century. The first was in 1904 at Lougher Bridge near Llanelly on the Great Western, where a saddle tank engine was acting as pilot to an express. On a long falling gradient, with the drawbar pull reduced to nil, the engine developed a roll, which was made progressively worse by the surging of water in the tank until finally it left the rails. Four lives were lost in this accident. The third was the derailment near Weedon in 1951, involving a tender engine, which I have already referred to briefly. The second was the accident to be described here. It took place about half a mile on the London side of Sevenoaks Tubs Hill station on August 24, 1927.

Among the bad summers of the century the villainous season of 1927 ranks high. It never seemed to stop raining. Such weather means an anxious time for the permanent way staff, for it seeks out any weaknesses in the track and demands constant vigilance by the maintenance gangs. So in this derailment at Sevenoaks we may name the weather as the chief culprit. But not, I think, the only one; the track itself was faulty. Was the locomotive design faulty too? It is that question which gives the accident its interest.

Among the pre-grouping Companies the South Eastern & Chatham was not one of the shining lights. An amalgam of two of the worst lines in Britain, the South Eastern and the London Chatham & Dover —which still retained their separate legal identities—it had only partly managed to outgrow two thoroughly bad traditions. Its rolling stock was poor and its trains were slow. Its boat trains in particular compared sadly with the brilliant performances of the Nord Company on the other side. Part of the trouble was shortage of money, and the shareholders of both constituent Companies were well-drilled not to expect dividends. Among other shortcomings was a somewhat inferior track, to which the local ballast material may have contributed. At the time of the accident the Company had been grouped for over four years into the Southern, but this is not long in which to effect radical improvements, especially to the road bed. This piece of track had been down for twenty-one years.

One of the Company's better features was its locomotives. These included some powerful 4-4-0s built in Germany and delivered not long before war broke out, while shortly afterwards a big step forward was taken in the decision to build a 2-6-4 express tank engine. No doubt the success of the neighbouring Brighton line in handling much of its fast traffic with tank engines had a bearing on the decision. The prototype, No. 790, appeared in 1917, but for some reason no more were built until after the grouping, in 1926, when they were named after south country streams and became known as the River class. Some had two outside cylinders and some three cylinders; for tank engines they had the large-sized coupled wheels of 6 feet diameter, which meant a high centre of gravity. We have noted that most locomotive derailments have involved tank engines, and this is no accident. Compared with a tender engine, a tank engine is inherently less stable, at all events at speed. The mere absence of a tender deprives it of one stabilizing influence, while the water in the tanks is liable to surge, despite the baffles. Moreover there is the problem of springing. Two million gallons of water weigh about nine tons, which means that the weight on each coupled axle could vary by as much as three tons. The River class was rather lightly sprung, an excellent feature for a good track, for it means the engine is less hard on the road. But the South Eastern & Chatham track, as I have said, was far from being in the top class. When the Rivers were multiplied the first batch was loaned to the Brighton section, where they performed with complete success, but back on their own section they were soon in trouble. Drivers complained of their rolling at speeds at above 50 m.p.h. It was noticed that the rolling tended to be worse in wet weather, and on certain stretches of the line. The two-cylinder engines, with their large 19 inches × 28 inches outside cylinders, were said to be particularly bad. It is hard to understand why this proclivity was not discovered while No. 790 was at work alone, but it was not, for whatever reason.

Nor was it merely a matter of rolling. There had been more than one actual derailment, though without serious consequences. In the previous March No. 890, River Frome, had come off the rails at Wrotham, while on August 2nd No. 800 had done likewise on a sharp curve at Maidstone. Only four days before the Sevenoaks accident No. 890 came off the road again with its whole train near Bearsted. It was travelling slowly and the train did not overturn, and no one was hurt. This accident was ascribed to track subsidence caused by rain. Most ominous of all, one of the class actually became derailed at speed, but miraculously re-railed itself. Only the tell-tale marks on the sleepers showed what had happened. In view of this run of mishaps it can hardly be said that the Sevenoaks accident came as a surprise.

August 24th was a typical 1927 summer's day. There were three storms over London; in Kent it rained all the morning, though it had stopped by two o'clock. On this day the 5 p.m. from Cannon Street to Minster via Deal, first stop Ashford, was in the charge of Driver Buss on No. 800, the engine which had come off the line at Maidstone three weeks before. It was hauling an eight-coach load, including a Pullman, well filled with returning City workers. Buss knew all about the River class and its rolling. Having breasted Knockholt summit at about 35 m.p.h. he was anxious, he said, to keep the speed of the train within limits on the four-mile descent to Dunton Green, which begins with over two miles through the Polhill tunnel at 1 in 143. At the same time he warned his fireman, who was new to the class, to put on some coal while in the tunnel, so as to avoid being thrown about the footplate as the train gathered speed. Rather surprisingly, Buss kept his regulator partly open right down to the foot of the bank, by which time the train was certainly travelling at more than 60 m.p.h., though Buss estimated only 57.

Dunton Green was a well-known rolling spot for these engines. This time the roll was thought to have been set up by trailing points beyond the station, and it became intensified as the train traversed the embankment which crosses the floor of the Darent valley. Then the engine crew heard an unusual knocking sound in front, which Buss supposed to have been caused by the leading Bissel truck having left the track. In fact the nearside leading coupled wheel had mounted the rail, on which the flange marks showed for 23 feet before they dropped over the side. The knocking was the sound of the wheel striking the chairs, and on hearing it Buss immediately closed his regulator. When the knocking still continued he applied the brake also.

At this point the gradient changes to 1 in 160 up, and the line enters a deep chalk cutting on a left-hand curve. Had this cutting been unobstructed Buss might well have been able to pull up his train on the rising gradient with no worse results than those at Bearsted four days before. Unfortunately a road bridge, known locally as the dark arch, spans the cutting at a skew angle with a pier between the rails, and this proved the fatal obstacle. By this time the engine was swaying violently; a passer-by who was on the bridge noticed that it seemed to be rolling about a foot to either side.

Many of the passengers on the train were regulars. They too knew about the Rivers' rolling propensities and on other journeys had been heard to say: 'We shall be off the line.' So as the coaches started rocking violently at least one passenger prepared himself for trouble. He was a Mr Fred Upton, of Folkestone. 'I knew there was going to be an accident,' he said, 'so I got down into a corner and stayed there with my feet up. "Put your feet up," I said to the other passengers, and they did so."' He was uninjured.

The partially-derailed No. 800 struck the bridge on both sides as it swayed. The left-hand cylinder and front corner of the engine struck the abutment, while the right-hand side of the cab scraped the centre pier. The engine ran on for over 100 yards further, taking the leading three coaches with it, and all came to rest leaning against the steep side of the cutting. The fourth coach was crushed and jammed under the arch, while the Pullman behind it was thrown broadside against the central pier. Strange to relate, no one in the Pullman was hurt. Thirteen passengers lost their lives, and the injured included Lord and Lady Lewisham and a former Lord Mayor of London, Sir Charles Wakefield, the oil magnate. The driver, Buss, escaped with cuts, but his fireman was unconscious for two days.

It was the first pair of coupled wheels which became derailed, not the Bissel truck carrying the pair of leading wheels. It might seem impossible for an intermediate pair of wheels to leave the rails like this, and under test the circumstances were only reproduced with difficulty. But the marks on the track proved that this had happened.

Which was to blame, the engine or the track? At the inquiry a ganger gave evidence that the section had been inspected just before the accident and was found to be in perfect order. We may take leave to ask what was meant on that line by perfect order, because it transpired that the superelevation on the curve was irregular and at one point was 1½ inches below its proper height. It appeared that owing to the number of bad spots caused by the weather maintenance had got into arrears.

Without waiting for the official report of the accident the Southern Railway withdrew the entire River class from service, an action which caused quite a sensation at the time. But at the Ministry inquiry the Chief Mechanical Engineer, Mr R. E. L. Maunsell, put up a spirited defence of the class, which he had designed. He did not agree that with tank engines there was more oscillation than with tender engines, though they gave a different kind of roll. The class had been withdrawn, he explained, to re-assure the public, but the Company was contemplating putting it back into service again. Engines of the same sort would still be designed in future; he saw no reason to make a change.

Brave words, but the Southern had second thoughts. Apart from compactness, there was no special advantage in using tank engines for expresses; since they always ran chimney first on fast trains they had to be turned just like tender engines. So in due course the class re-appeared as tender engines, in which form they gave no trouble.

Before that happened Mr Maunsell sought to vindicate his design, and invoked the assistance of his opposite number Gresley, the celebrated Chief Mechanical Engineer of the London & North Eastern. One of the class was tried out on the former Great Northern main line between Huntingdon and St Neots, and ran up to 85 m.p.h. without developing any dangerous roll. A further test on the London & South Western line between Woking and Walton had less happy results. A Southern King Arthur class 4-6-0 was included in the tests, and Gresley noted that both the tank and the tender engines rolled excessively at speeds of over 70. As on the South Eastern & Chatham section, the rolling always occurred in the same places, thus proving that it was due to the track.

Who or what then was really to blame? No individual, surely, but rather a common weakness of railway organization, at all events in the past; a lack of liaison between the locomotive and the engineer's departments. There are several instances of where a new type of locomotive has fallen under the engineering department's ban and has had to be modified, or restricted in its range of routes, simply because the locomotive department did not take the precaution of finding out beforehand. In this case Maunsell ought to have known, or found out, that his otherwise excellent design was unsuitable for the track it had to run on. As it was, the fact had to be established by a series of mishaps culminating in a disaster.

One party, however, must have derived satisfaction out of the episode. This was the L.N.E.R., whose Great Northern main line was proved to be what it had always claimed to be, one of the best-laid tracks in the world.

CHAPTER 14

DARLINGTON

LONDON & NORTH EASTERN
RAILWAY

Most of the drivers concerned in these accidents were elderly men in their fifties and sixties. This is the story of a young driver, whose inexperience proved his undoing. He was not a regular driver but a passed fireman, meaning one who has qualified as a driver but has not yet been upgraded. He was thirty-two.

I speak of inexperience, but whether it was inexperience alone that led to the collision at Darlington on the night of June 27, 1928, or a strange self-delusion as well, the reader must judge for himself.

Passed fireman Bell, a Gateshead man, had done a good deal of driving of the sort that his kind expect: taking light engines to and from the sheds, working local freights and the like. On this occasion he was called upon to deputize for the regular man on a main line turn, the 9.30 p.m. semi-fast from Newcastle to Darlington, which continued as a parcels-only train to York. At Darlington it usually did some shunting to add or detach vehicles. Bell had traversed the road to York many times as a fireman and once before as a driver, and though he had not been called upon to sign the Road Book, an acknowledgement that he knew the road and signals, he said that he was quite prepared to do so. But knowledge of the road is one thing and knowledge of the sidings is quite another, and in all his journeys Bell had never had to shunt in Darlington station. As he put it: 'A man might go ten years between Newcastle and Darlington and know nothing of the "middle road" '—the track next to the platform line which figures in our story.

Bank Top station, Darlington, is looped off the main line to the west, on the down side, that is. It consists of a wide island platform with bay platforms at either end. On both up and down sides of the island, in addition to the platform line, are two additional through lines known to railwaymen as the middle and back roads. The back road does not come into the story, except in so far as its existence may have helped to confuse Bell. Signalling at that time was of the ordinary semaphore pattern, with smaller 'calling-on' arms underneath the main arms for shunting purposes.

The layout was (and is) somewhat cramped, in that the distance between the point of convergence of the platform, middle and back roads and the main line points at the South Junction is only forty-eight yards. Therefore any train longer than that wanting to shunt from one of the three roads to another has to run onto the main line. It can either run across onto the up main line or onto the down line by means of a slip. In either case it fouls the down main line, so that shunting has to be suspended when a down non-stopping train is due.

On this evening Bell reached Darlington at 10.45, eleven minutes late, in charge of ex-N.E. 4-6-0 No. 2369. He drew up at the north end of the platform, but was signalled forward to the south end in order to make room for another train. Standing in the middle road was a rake of seven vans, which were to be included in the train behind the third van. Shunter Morland uncoupled between the third and fourth vehicles and told Bell that he was to run up to the South Junction and back onto the middle road to pick up the seven vans. Since Bell had forty-five yards of engine and vans, this meant running out onto the main line in order to clear the points and get back on to the platform road. In the normal course a simple forward-and-back shunt requires a single signal only, and so would this one have done if it had not involved fouling the main line. As it was, two signals were required. Directly ahead of Bell was the small calling-on-signal No. 8, which gave him permission to move as far as Signal No. 18, the middle road starter 100 yards ahead, which protected the main line. Signal No. 8 was duly lowered, and Bell moved forward. But an excursion from Scarborough to Newcastle was due to pass on the down main line, so signal No. 18 remained at danger. Bell however had managed to convince himself that signal No. 8 gave him permission to complete his shunt, and though No. 18 was on a gantry of three, all at danger, he ran past it and on to the main line.

How did Bell come so to delude himself? He himself was at a loss to explain. Even granted his ignorance of the signalling, and if he was not quite certain which signal was his, it seems extraordinary that he should run past a group of three, all of them at danger. Looking back now, we can perhaps suggest how the confusion may have arisen in his mind. In the first place there was the unusual circumstance of a second signal being involved in the shunt. In the second place, while Signal No. 8 was on Bell's right, the entire gantry on which No. 18 stood was on his left. With the back road on his left side also, and other lines beyond, he may have persuaded himself that none of the three referred to the middle road. Bell himself said that he was misled by a similar case of signalling at Newcastle, but this one turned out on examination to be different. It appeared, though, that other enginemen before Bell had found the signalling here confusing. A shouted explanation from the Station East signal box, close to which Bell's engine was standing, might have put things right, but signalmen were loth to trust a verbal message against the noise of the engines.

So Bell, in all innocence, was away out onto the main line. An alarmed Morland, riding on the third van, saw him pass signal No. 18 and lifted the brake tap in the van. Morland did not apply the brake fully, he explained, for fear of breaking the train. The train had slowed down to a walking pace when Morland heard a whistle. 'He's "got the boards",' he thought—clear signals—and released the brake. But he was wrong; it was the approaching excursion train which had whistled. He looked out again. He was nearly level with Signal No. 18, which was still at danger. He applied the brake again, and had brought the train nearly to a standstill when the collision occurred.

Signalman Garrett in the South Junction box, all unaware of Bell's foray onto the main line, had set the road for the excursion. Then, like Gibson and Clark at Hull, he heard a curious clicking noise in the level frame. It was Bell's train running through two sets of trailing points set against him. Garrett did not know this, but the noise spelt something amiss, and he threw the down signals to danger. Too late.

Driver McNulty, in charge of ex-N.E.R. Class Z Atlantic No. 2164, at the head of eleven coaches on the excursion, was travelling at about 45 m.p.h. as he approached South Junction signal box. At the down home signals just beyond he saw the lights of Bell's engine running in from the left onto his road, not more than fifty yards away. He reacted with lightning speed. With only two or three seconds to act he had no time to use sand or reverse his engine. He applied his Westinghouse brake, which was just beginning to bite when the two engines met head-on.

Shrewsbury. Experiment class no. 2052, 'Stephenson', lying where it ended its disastrous journey with the mangled remains of most of its complement of carriages heaped up behind. The impression of the coach on top is that it was made from rather inferior matchwood. Note the tender devoid of coal. (*Radio Times Hulton Picture Library*)

Salisbury. A view of the clearing-up operations looking towards London across the Fisherton Street Bridge. The eight-wheeled 'Watercart' tender of the L12 can be clearly seen in the middle of the wreckage, whilst the top of the chimney of the Beyer Peacock goods locomotive is just visible in front of the telegraph pole at the far end of the carriage top. (*Illustrated London News*)

Below. Zig-zagged coaches of the Newtown to Welshpool Express which plunged head on into the west-bound slow train causing 15 deaths on the single line of the Cambrian Railway. *(National Railway Museum).*

Top left. Hull Paragon. Γ class no. 96 on the right, locked with its fellow 4-4-0 as if in deadly combat. *(Illustrated London News)*

Below right. Norton Fitzwarren. The stricken King class no. 6028, renamed after the reigning monarch 'King George VI', with the wreckage of the worse damaged coaches behind it covering the crucial catch-points. The flooded conditions through which Driver Stacey waded waist deep are well in evidence here and must have hindered the rescue work too. Now, with the casualties taken away, it is a time for assessment and investigation. *(Photosource)*

Castlecary. Seen from the other side, only the tender of 'Grand Parade' can be clearly distinguished. Some idea is gained here of the terrible power of the momentum that sent the train's first two carriages shooting over the engine leaving the third perched on top. *(Photosource)*

Sevenoaks. Pullman car 'Carmen' rammed broadside across the Shireham Lane overbridge. Seeing the state of it here makes it seem all the more remarkable that none of its occupants was hurt. As in other accidents, the superior construction of Pullman vehicles was, no doubt, largely responsible for that. Imagine what would have happened to most of the other coaches seen in pictures on previous pages. *(Radio Times Hulton Picture Library)*

Bourne End. With the carriages removed, the mutilated hulk of no. 6157, 'The Royal Artilleryman', having been righted, is lifted out of the field – a difficult and delicate task for the crane-crew. 'The Royal Scot' is a sad contrast to the Class S locomotive heading the recovery train behind. (H. C. Casserley)

Winsford. Duchess Pacific no. 6251, 'City of Nottingham' lies with steam still rising in the middle of the two wrecked trains. Its leading coach, which was a GWR milk van – an odd component of a postal train – stands behind the tender surprisingly intact but little else of the train remains identifiable. Between the carriage in the foreground and the locomotive is all that is left of the two vehicles in which the passenger deaths occurred. (Illustrated London News)

A night photograph taken soon after the collision of the little-damaged engine of the second train, later able to steam away, entwined with the wreckage of the rear coach of the first train into which it crashed. *(Illustrated London News)*

Lewisham. Just how devastating an effect the bridge collapse had on the second coach can be seen here after much of the debris has been removed. The still dangerous bridge has been propped up and screens erected to shield the more gruesome and tragic discoveries from the curiosity of the inevitable sightseers. *(Photosource)*

Quintinshill. In this newspaper picture the intensity of the fire gives some idea of the horror of the holocaust. *(Illustrated London News)*

Harrow. Duchess Pacific no. 46242, 'City of Glasgow', which headed the Scottish express and ran into the back of the local, after two days of salvage efforts had uncovered it from under the forty-foot high pile of wreckage. Hardly recognisable as a locomotive any more, the front right hand driving wheel and leading bogies can be seen in the centre of the picture. *(Associated Press)*.

Replacing 2-4-0 Precedent class 'COOK' on the rails following the crash which resulted in 15 deaths. *(Radio Times Hulton Picture Library)*

Lewisham. The end of the Hayes train about to be lifted free of Battle of Britain class light Pacific no. 34066, 'Spitfire', which is still rammed into it. The motor coach at the rear of the ten car electric train has survived the collision remarkably well, but the eighth coach was almost totally destroyed after being overridden by the ninth as can be glimpsed in the background. Despite this, and bearing in mind that each carriage was carrying about 150 people, the toll of thirty-seven passengers killed in the suburban train seems miraculously light. *(Photosource)*

Bell had seen the lights of the excursion at just about the same time. He had the presence of mind to release his brakes in order to lessen the shock.

Bell's engine was driven back sixty yards along the down main line. It was not derailed, but it had its buffer beam knocked off and was otherwise badly damaged. The first four vans behind it were totally destroyed. No. 2164 of the excursion, likewise minus its buffer beam, ran forward for sixty-five yards before overturning on its left side, with its tender broken loose behind it. All the coaches of the excursion train remained upright, but the underframe of the third coach cut into five crowded compartments of the second—a non-corridor—and no one in these escaped death or injury. The leading coach—the only one—was gaslit, but the cylinder was not broken and there was no fire.

Twenty-five passengers lost their lives and forty-five were seriously injured, as were both drivers and the firemen of the excursion. How Morland riding on the third van escaped annihilation is a mystery, but he did, and I learned in Darlington that he is still alive.

Twenty of the dead were women, fourteen of them on a Mothers' Union outing from the colliery township of Hetton-le-Hole. To Hetton it was like a pit disaster with widowers instead of widows; there were four in a single street.

The inquiry, which was conducted by Col. Pringle, gave rise to a flicker of animosity between the railway Unions. The General Secretary of the locomotive men's Union, Mr John Bromley, tried to put the responsibility for the accident onto Signalman Robson in the Station East box—a man with fifty years' experience who does not come into our story because he acted correctly throughout. Col. Pringle cut Mr Bromley short. 'There is no responsibility on this man,' he said.

The primary fault quite clearly lay with Bell. His knowledge of signalling, the Colonel concluded, was insufficient to enable him to read the signals of a strange yard correctly; he should have sought information from Morland. But Bell was commended for the straightforward way in which he had given his evidence. Morland had also had to bear a share of the blame, in that he should have acted more resolutely and applied the brake to the full when he saw Bell overrunning the signal. Driver McNulty of the excursion train was absolved from all blame, as were all the signalmen concerned.

It seems to me that there was a point in Morland's defence which was not brought out at the inquiry. He must have known by heart the times of all the regular trains passing on the main line. If the excursion had been an ordinary scheduled train, Morland would have known it was due and would certainly have brought Bell to a stop. But he was not to know anything about a special.

As for signalling, Col. Pringle suggested the substitution of a single three-aspect colour light signal for each of the three lines, which would show yellow when the signal ahead was at danger. Even the most inexperienced man could not possibly misunderstand this. In due course, eleven years later, this recommendation was carried out and the whole of Darlington station converted to colour-light signalling.

The Colonel also had a word to say about the value of buck-eye couplers in preventing telescoping. The L.N.E.R. adopted these later as standard, and we shall see how their value was proved in later accidents. Finally he repeated, with wearisome re-iteration, that the accident could have been prevented by automatic train control. This recommendation had become almost standard form in cases where a driver was at fault, but its implementation was still nearly thirty years away.

So ends the story of the young driver who came to grief. It is not the end of the calamitous story of 1928. Besides a whole series of lesser accidents, a further spectacular and terrible catastrophe was to occur before the year was out. That is described in the next chapter.

CHAPTER 15

CHARFIELD

LONDON MIDLAND & SCOTTISH RAILWAY

The year 1928 was the worst for accidents in the history of the grouped Companies. In its first ten months there were no less than thirteen accidents involving deaths, in which fifty-seven lives were lost. They included the two major accidents at Darlington, described in the last chapter, and Charfield, to be described here. By a strange coincidence both disasters involved trains shunting. At Charfield a Great Western goods train, backing into a lie-by siding, was run into by an L.M.S. night Mail which had run past three signals at danger. It happened at about 5.20 in the morning of Saturday, October 13th.

Of all the accidents recorded in this book, Charfield is the most romantic, if one can apply such a term to a disaster. Its human stories are among the most interesting, while it is alleged to contain a mystery. Moreover I have been able to talk to some of the local participants, a surprising number of whom are still alive. Their accounts throw fresh light on the occurrence.

Let us now introduce the main characters. First, Driver Aldington of the Mail and his fireman Want, of Bournville shed. Aldington, a man of sixty, reminds us of Martin at Shrewsbury: a corpulent man who was fond of his pint, or ought I to say pints. Unlike Martin however he had an exemplary record, which included an award for vigilance. Of Want it must be said that, whatever his errors on this occasion, he was a first-class fireman. Only an expert could have built a fire sufficient to keep that engine with that load going so fast up-hill. Then the two signalmen: Harry Smith at Berkeley Road, now living in sprightly and active retirement at Charfield, and Harry Button, an older man, in Charfield box.

Charfield station, now closed, lies on the former Midland Company's Derby to Bristol main line between the also-closed stations of

Berkeley Road Junction and Wickwar. Over the stretch between Standish Junction near Stonehouse and Yate the Great Western exercised running powers, not at all to the liking of the Midland who had to accommodate a competitor, which is how a Great Western train came to be involved.

Just before 5 a.m. on this morning the situation was as follows. Shunted onto the branch line at Berkeley Road was a Great Western semi-fitted goods consisting of forty-nine loaded vehicles and a brake van hauled by 2-6-0 No. 6381. Ahead of it, in the lie-by at Charfield, was an L.M.S. unfitted goods. This had picked up six loaded coal trucks at Berkeley Road and was now overloaded for the Class 3 0-6-0 hauling it. Both these trains had been shunted to allow a passage for a parcels train from Leicester, which had now gone through. Coming up behind was the night Mail from Leeds to Bristol, with through postal vans from Newcastle, which had left Gloucester at 4.54.

Which goods should now have priority, the overburdened L.M.S. train in front, or the faster-running Great Western one behind? On other lines the question would have been settled by the signalmen on the spot. But the Midland had a system of centralized train control, which had been taken over by the L.M.S. and by which the area controller took such decisions. It had been introduced to speed up goods traffic, and though it certainly had done that, it was said to be sometimes rather rigid in its operation. I now come to a circumstance which was not brought out at the inquiry, but which is vouched for by Signalman Smith. As it had an indirect bearing on the accident it seems relevant to mention it. The men on the ground, Button and Smith, advised that the Great Western train should go forward and the other one stay shunted at Charfield until both the Great Western and the Mail had passed. The Great Western could then have reached its own line at Yate Junction and got clear out of the way, whereas to send the L.M.S. forward was bound to cause delays. However the controller at Fishponds decided otherwise. He was a man, says Smith, who had been dismissed from Control during the war for the serious blunder of holding up an ambulance train, but had managed to get himself reinstated. One sees in him the typical rigid-minded functionary of the sort which had caused criticism of the system. So the L.M.S. goods was sent on and there was no choice, short of delaying the Mail, to putting the Great Western train, when it reached Charfield, into the lie-by which the other had just vacated. The L.M.S.

driver, however, decided without warning to take water, so delaying the Great Western train still further, before dragging his way up the hill to Wickwar.

At this time, about an hour before dawn, a ground mist was beginning to rise. It was specially thick between the distant and outer home signals, where the line went from embankment to cutting. The train crews said afterwards that the fogmen should have been called out, but Button maintained that he had kept sight of his fog object, the back light of the down inner home signal, 214 yards away. In the case of a ground mist a driver's-eye-view may be very different from a signalman's, moreover the thickest patch was out of sight of the box. But it is doubtful if the mist had any real bearing on the accident.

The system of signalling at Charfield was (and still is) the one standard on the Midland main lines, known as the 'rotary interlocking' block. The effect of this is that no train can be signalled into the block in advance until the train ahead has operated a release treadle at the next box, and the signalman there has accepted the second train on his block instrument. At Charfield, additionally, when the points were set for the lie-by normal interlocking prevented the inner and outer home signals, and therefore the distant, from being pulled off. At the outer home signal was a track circuit.

The Great Western train duly arrived at Charfield, and Button called out to the driver that it was to be shunted into the lie-by. He set the points, and slowly Driver Gilbert began to back his fifty-vehicle train off the main line. It had operated the release treadle before coming to a halt, thus enabling Smith at Berkeley Road to offer the Mail, which was now approaching that station. Button cleared back the goods at 5.13 and immediately accepted the Mail, which he was entitled to do under the regulations. His distant and both his home signals were locked at danger by reason of the points being set for the lie-by; this meant that the Mail would first be checked at the distant and then come to a stand at the outer home signal—on the track circuit—until the goods was clear of the main line.

The Mail, in charge of the corpulent Aldington, was hauled by Johnson Class 3 4-4-0 No. 714, rebuilt with superheater: a class which had a life-span of over half a century and for many years bore the brunt of the express work between Derby and Bristol. Its train of eleven vehicles contained only four passenger coaches, marshalled at Nos. 3 to 6, and carrying a night Mail's usual light load of about sixty passengers. Such secondary expresses are not held to warrant the most modern stock, and the passenger coaches varied in age from nineteen to twenty-nine years. Three out of the four were gas-lit, as well as five of the vans; the Midland's policy of conversion to electric lighting had made rather half-hearted progress in the fifteen years since Ais Gill.

The down line had recently been relaid between Berkeley Road and Mangotsfield, and a 45-m.p.h. restriction was still in force. Aldington, however—though he denied it later—kept going at about 60 m.p.h. It was good travelling, one must agree, against the rising trend of the road. Aldington was probably trying to recoup a four minutes' late start from Gloucester. There was nothing dangerous in such a speed, but it chanced that the minute or so gained precipitated the accident.

Here is Aldington's story of what happened next, as he told it at the inquiry. It was foggy in patches, he said. Approaching the Charfield distant he crossed over to the left side of the cab and was able to read it at eighty yards' distance, when it was showing a clear green. Fireman Want, too, though unused to the road, saw the signal at sixty yards and called out: 'He's got it off, mate.' Between the distant and the outer home the fog became thicker, but with the distant at clear (said Aldington) he carried on with the regulator open, though he admitted missing both home signals. He had never been checked at Charfield before, and would be expecting a clear run. Is this yet another instance of a railwayman's imagination leading him astray? Signalman Smith, who saw a good deal of Aldington in the days following the crash, does not think so. His view is that Aldington had become drowsy, possibly as the result of a few drinks before starting out, and had dozed off—as we have supposed happened to Martin at Shrewsbury—so that he saw no signals at all. As for the fireman, as Smith puts it, he would hardly know whether he was at Berkeley Road, Charfield or Wickwar.

Button at Charfield was watching his track circuit indicator. He saw it change to 'occupied' as the Mail reached it. Then to his consternation it changed back to 'clear'. With the goods still not clear of the main line, the Mail had run through his signals. In agony Button clutched his head in his hands, awaiting the calamity he could do nothing to prevent.

Driver Gilbert had practically finished propelling his train into the lie-by. Ten seconds later and the whole train would have been safely stowed away. But at Charfield every circumstance was un-lucky. The two leading wagons were still on the points when No. 714 caught them and then struck the back of the Great Western engine's tender. If the collision had taken place on an open stretch the results would have been serious enough. But just where the lie-by diverged there is a substantial brick overbridge to constrict the space. By a further evil chance an L.M.S. up empty goods train was passing at that moment. No. 714 bounced off the Great Western tender, which overturned to the left, and shot across the tracks to the right, where it drove through seven or eight of the empty goods wagons before coming to rest leaning against the cutting side. Its tender, the Great Western engine, and the smashed trucks became wedged together in a compact mass under the bridge. Against this solid obstacle the Mail's five leading vehicles piled themselves in a tangle of wreckage. The fifth vehicle—one of the passenger coaches—was forced up against the side of the bridge and part of its roof shot into the road-way. The scene at Ditton Junction sixteen years before was re-enacted, as was the dread sequel.

Sixteen passengers died in the disaster. Some of the dead—probably most—were killed instantly. One woman passenger was catapulted to her death clean over the bridge to land in a truck on the far side. A man was hurled dying on to the roadway. Of the rest we cannot be sure, for within minutes the wreckage had become a fur-nace. A cloud of gas from the broken cylinders was ignited either by coals from the engine or sparks, and was fed by more gas escaping from fractured connections. The Bristol fire brigade was on the scene in thirty-five minutes, and water was pumped from a stream several hundred yards away, but as we have seen, against a gas-fed fire water is helpless. The first six vehicles of the Mail, including all four pas-senger coaches, were burned out, together with the two front wagons of the goods train with all their contents and a number of empty wagons.

I have said that the death-roll was sixteen. That is the official num-ber, and it is probably correct. But the deaths of two men passengers had to be presumed; they were known to be on the train and were never heard of again, nor was any trace found of them or their belongings. Just as at Hawes Junction, the dead were incinerated; two members of the Coroner's jury described to me the gruesome business of inspecting the remains. In most cases a charred fragment of bone or clothing provided the only clue.

Both Aldington and Want had miraculous escapes, but the guard of the Mail, Millier, was less lucky. He was travelling in the rear van, the only vehicle to remain undamaged, but he was thrown forward by the shock and dislocated his shoulder. The Post Office sorters came off badly too. Their vans were behind the passenger coaches and kept the rails, but thirteen of them were injured, as were both the Great Western enginemen.

Half an hour after the accident Aldington went up into the signal box. The distant, he told Button, was off. 'Impossible,' replied Button. Aldington pointed to the repeater: sure enough it was showing 'off'. But that furnished no backing for his story. It was found that wreckage had fallen on the wire and driven it right into the ground, thus pulling the repeater into the 'off' position. The Inspecting Officer, Col. Sir John Pringle, who appears here for the last time, investigated every possibility that might have caused the distant to be showing Clear, including the chance that some article from the goods train might have fallen on to the wire. But he could find nothing. Short of the fantastic assumption of some nocturnal practical joker, the case was proved.

So Col. Pringle brushed aside Aldington's story, as he had brushed aside Gourlay's at Elliot Junction twenty-two years before. He said straight out that he did not accept it, and held Aldington responsible for the crash, and in a lesser degree the fireman, Want, whom he described as not a reliable witness.

In the meantime the inquest had been held. The two ex-jurymen told me that Aldington gave his evidence in a straightforward manner, but the jury did not believe him any more than the Inspector had done. They held that the collision had been caused by his negligence, which the Coroner interpreted as a verdict of manslaughter. With the Ais Gill inquest in mind I asked if the jury had intended it that way, and the answer was yes.

Aldington appeared before the magistrates at Wotton-under-Edge. His Union had briefed Sir Henry Curtis Bennett, K.C., one of the most famous Counsel of the day, in his defence. Sir Henry tried hard to extract an admission from the Company's officers that the distant might have been showing Clear. He had no success. But at what point does negligence become criminal? The magistrates took only five minutes to decide that there was no case to answer, and Aldington was formally acquitted at the Gloucester Assizes. He was luckier,

we may think, than Caudle at Ais Gill, who was far less blameworthy.

So Aldington departed to Bournville, to spend the remainder of
his driving days on shunting engines.

Back for a moment to Signalman Button, who had had to wait
helplessly for the crash. The sequel is something I should not dare to
set down had I not had it from Signalman Smith at first hand. I give
it as nearly as may be in Smith's own words:

'I saw Button (he says) on the Sunday, the day after the accident.
There was nothing unusual about him then. When I next saw him a
few days later his black hair was streaked with white. "Have you put
your head in a white paint pot, Harry?" I asked. "No, my boy", he
replied, "that's where I put my hands on the top of my head when
I saw the crash was coming. It's the result of the shock just coming
out."'

Button's hair regained its normal colour after about a couple of
years. But who says it is just a myth that people's hair can turn white
from shock?

Such is the story of Charfield, the last of the great fire disasters. By
the time of our next accident, seven years on, the railways had passed
out of the gas-lighting age.

Up on the hill at Old Charfield, where the pitiful, derelict church
presides over an unkempt graveyard, stands the L.M.S. Company's
memorial to the dead, kept trim by railwaymen and inmates of the
Leyhill open prison nearby. Twelve of the victims are buried there,
and in the centre appears the legend: 'Two Unknown'.

Who were they? This is the famous Mystery of the Charfield
Children, which appeared again in print only recently. The story
goes that the bodies of two children were found in the wreckage, too
charred to be recognizable; that they could not be connected with
any of the other victims and that no one came forward to claim
them. They are said to be the two in the Unknowns' grave.

I have probed this story with the help of the records and local
residents. Its origin is as follows. The porter who examined the
tickets on the train at Gloucester recalled seeing two children, a boy
of about twelve and a girl of nine, or so he thought, travelling together in school uniform and each clutching their ticket as if they
had no grown-up with them. Among the charred remains was a boy's
jacket with the motto: 'Luce Magistra' and a tape tab bearing the

name: G. S. S. Saunders, together with a 15½ size stiff collar with the initials G.S.S.S. Also a fragment of footwear identified by the local doctor as probably belonging to a girl. On the strength of these relics it was assumed that the two unknown dead were the child travellers.

I have spoken to Mr Fred Ayres, who is still active and at work and who put the remains, such as they were, into the coffins. 'Some of them you could have put into a matchbox', he says. He tells me that the sole contents of the two Unknowns' coffins are in each case a charred piece of footwear—whether shoe, slipper or the then-popular Russian boot it was impossible to say—together with a little ash, which may or may not be human. There was nothing that led him to suppose that either remains might be those of children. It seems as if the doctor in the confusion of the moment made a wrong identification and afterwards did not like to admit it.

There *were* two children on the train. Their names were Moyra and Eric Wade, aged thirteen and eleven, who were travelling with their mother. The girl was badly injured, but all survived. There can be little doubt that they were the children seen by the porter.

Charfield station looks forlorn now, but the line is as busy as ever. The two lie-byes—there was one on the up line as well—were converted into loops during the war, so that fact alone would prevent a recurrence of the accident. The distant signal which Aldington missed has been replaced by an outer distant colour light and an inner distant carried on the same post, unusually, as the outer home that protects the entrance to the loop. More track circuits have been installed, and their lights wink on a vast track diagram that fills half the rear of the box. Only some newer brickwork on the bridge parapet, and the memorial on the hill, remain as reminders of Charfield's dawn of horror.

CHAPTER 16

WELWYN GARDEN CITY

LONDON & NORTH EASTERN RAILWAY

This is the story of an inadequate personality; of a signalman who was not up to his job. In some other of these accidents we may suspect that if the signalman had been a little brighter or more alert there would have been no disaster. This is the only case in which it was said officially, in so many words, that he was not a suitable man to be in that box.

Signalman Shaw, as I will call him, was no novice. He had had twenty-three years' experience, and Welwyn Garden City was his fourth box. His last had been at Doncaster, a one-direction box with some permissive block working. Welwyn was his first No. 1 box, and he had been chosen for it by seniority rather than by merit. The stationmaster at Welwyn described him as 'an almost peculiarly quiet man; difficult to get anything out of him', while his instructor had noted that he had taken five weeks to learn the working of the box. A rather dim type, we might say, perhaps with a chip on his shoulder.

Welwyn Garden City is an unusually busy box. The four-track main line is flanked on either side by the single-line branches to Dunstable and Hertford, which though their junction point with the main line is at Hatfield only part company from it at Welwyn, so that the signalman there has (or had) three routes and six tracks to look after. The branch lines have no bearing on our story, but they meant that Welwyn more than usually was a box requiring a man who could keep his head at busy times, and Shaw was not such a one.

Shaw had not been in the box on his own for a week before he was in trouble. It was quite a small incident; he had pulled off the inner home signal too soon and allowed the driver to overrun the outer home at danger. It would have passed off with a mild reproof for a new man, but Shaw somehow managed to get in touch with the driver and to compound with him to hush it up. When it came to light, and the stationmaster ordered Shaw to make a report, he refused. So he found himself on the carpet at Kings Cross, not for the original error but for indiscipline, and received a severe reprimand, which was to be entered in his record. On the night of June 15, 1935, when he came on duty for the 10 o'clock shift, awaiting him in the box was confirmation of the reprimand in writing. In cold typescript the words seemed even more frightening than they had done verbally. Whether the state of mind they engendered had any effect on Shaw's actions a little over an hour later can only be conjectured, but it is at least possible that brooding resentment helped to take his mind off his work. We may think it tactless of the Company to hand such a document to a man just starting his night shift.

It was a Saturday night, and the 10.45 from Kings Cross to Newcastle was being run in two parts. The first train, No. 825, left at the scheduled time. The second part, train No. 825A, which was to take the coastal route via Sunderland, left at 10.53, well filled with 280 passengers and hauled by one of the famous Ivatt Atlantics, No. 4441. Behind it, at 10.58, came train No. 826, the newspaper express to Leeds due away at 10.50, with three passenger coaches among its eleven vehicles carrying fifty-seven passengers and hauled by 2-6-0 No. 4009, one of Gresley's powerful K3 class, with nearly double the Atlantic's tractive effort though not weighing a great deal more.

I shall refer to the trains by their numbers.

We pick up the story again at 11.20 in Hatfield No. 3 box, where Signalman Crowe, who had been in the box for eighteen out of his thirty-four years' service, had received Train Out Of Section from Shaw at Welwyn for train 825. The trains had been bunching up somewhat, and Crowe had already been offered No. 825A from Hatfield No. 1 box, which he offered forward to Welwyn, where it was accepted. He sent Train Entering Section for 825A to Welwyn as it passed his box at 11.22.

Over now to Welwyn box, where there had been a slight distraction. A parcel had been left in a train from Hertford, and some time before this the porter on duty had asked Shaw to phone Hatfield about it; apparently he could not do so himself. Now, at 11.22, Shaw's phone rang with the porter on the line a second time: could he please phone Hatfield about that parcel? As he had already received Train Entering Section from Hatfield for 825A, Shaw's duty should have been to pull off his signals for it, but for whatever reason—do we perceive a bit of cussedness here?—he made the call about the parcel first. In consequence he was late in clearing his signals. Driver Morris on No. 4441, seeing the distant at caution, supposed he was running into the signals of No. 825. He shut off steam and applied the brakes. He had reduced speed to about 15 m.p.h. when he saw the home signal go off as Shaw tardily got down to pulling his levers. Still supposing he was on the heels of train 825, Morris allowed his train to roll on towards the starter. Seeing it was clear he 'popped' his whistle and put on steam again. Almost immediately he felt a violent impact as No. 826 crashed into his rear.

Back to Crowe in Hatfield No. 3 box. One minute had passed, and it was now 11.23. To his surprise, Crowe received the Train Out Of Section signal from Shaw for 825A—a 2½-mile section apparently traversed in one minute. He had just been offered train No. 826 from Hatfield No. 1, which he offered forward to Shaw, who accepted it at once. That seemed to Crowe, as he put it, a bit smart, so he picked up the phone and asked Shaw: 'Is that out, Fred?' 'Yes,' came the reply. No. 826 passed his box at 11.25 and he sent Train Entering Section to Welwyn. At 11.29 he received the Danger Obstruction signal from Shaw. He picked up the phone again. 'No. 826 has run into the rear of 825A' Shaw told him. Crowe: 'But you gave Train Out Of Section for 825A at 11.23.' There was no reply.

Shaw had wrongly checked one train, wrongly given Line Clear and wrongly accepted another, all in the space of a few minutes. No wonder the Inspecting Officer thought him unsuitable to be in a No. 1 box.

Driver Barnes of Train 826, on his K3, was going well up the 1 in 200 gradient at 65 m.p.h. with the Welwyn signals showing green. But just as they came to the home signal his fireman shouted 'On'; it had changed to red. Beyond it Barnes saw the tail light on 825A 300 or 400 yards ahead. Once again we have to ask ourselves whether instantaneous action might not have prevented or reduced the accident. It was the same situation as at Hawes Junction: a fast-moving train closing in on a slower-moving one, this time at a net speed of about 50 m.p.h. This would have decreased fast as train 825A gathered speed and 826 braked. It was shown after the Castle-cary accident, to be described in our next chapter, that a train travelling on the level at 58 m.p.h. could be brought to a standstill in 478 yards. At Welwyn, even if the distance was less, so was the speed, while 826 was on a rising gradient. Partly no doubt it is the element of surprise which accounts for these relatively slow reactions; on the railway an accident practically never happens. The wise car driver is on the alert for trouble every moment of his journey; the engine driver clearly is not. That makes the occasional lightning reaction, like McNulty's at Darlington, all the more creditable. I need hardly say that Driver Barnes was not held in any degree responsible for the accident.

Train 826's speed must still have been high at the moment of impact, for the results were spectacular. The K3 drove right through the last coach of 825A, the frame of which was festooned about the engine. The coach bogies, and those of the coach in front of it, were driven forward 140 yards. No passengers in the last coach, nor the guard, survived. Including the guard, fourteen persons were killed. Extraordinary to relate, No. 4009 kept the rails.

Equally spectacular, but in a favourable way, was the behaviour of the buck-eye couplings with which some of the vehicles in both trains were fitted. In the seven years since the Darlington collision the L.N.E.R. had taken heed of the Inspector's advice, and the results were shown now in the remarkably low death-roll, for such a violent crash, among a combined passenger complement of over 300. In train No. 825A the last coach but one was an all-steel vehicle fitted with buck-eye couplings and shock-absorbing buffers. Both its bogies were pushed forward as I have described, but the coupling in front held fast and supported the body, and no one in it was seriously injured.

In train No. 826 the contrast was remarkable between the two types of coupling. The first three vehicles had buck-eye couplings, all of which held. The first vehicle, a van, partially telescoped into the engine's tender, but in the second not a pane of glass was broken. As showing how capricious are the effects of an accident, though the couplings in the third vehicle held, a number of passengers in it were seriously injured, doubtless by the shock of the impact. The six vehicles at Nos. 4 to 9, with ordinary screw couplings, were wrecked, but the last two with buck-eye couplings were not damaged.

Clearly the accident had been due to Shaw's wrong acceptance of train 826. What had happened, it transpired at the inquiry, was that he had got mixed up between the two Newcastle trains, 825 and

825A. He had forgotten that he had already given Train Out Of Section for No. 825 at 11.20, and had imagined that the train he acepted at 11.23 was No. 825A. There was no entry in his Train Book for the acceptance of No. 826. He had been passing an up train at the same time, and the Inspecting Officer, Col. Mount, thought he had got thoroughly confused, and had been giving and receiving signals and pegging trains on the wrong set of instruments.

But Shaw was far from accepting the penitent's role. He tried to throw the blame on to Crowe at Hatfield, which we may think was wholly in character. In the face of the evidence, he maintained that his Train Out Of Section signal referred to No. 825, and he thought Crowe was referring to that when he rang and asked: 'Is that out?'

It was no thanks to Shaw, but out of the Welwyn disaster came something good. The Inspecting Officer put his finger on a weak spot in the safety arrangements, and made a suggestion which was to have far-reaching results. I quote from the official report:

'As 825A had not reached the track circuit (200 yards long) in rear of the home signal when the second acceptance was given (for 826), apparently the accident would have been prevented had the controls on the block instruments by this track circuit been such that, once Line Clear had been transmitted, it could not have been transmitted a second time until the track circuit had been occupied and cleared.'

This system was widely adopted on the L.N.E.R. It became known as the 'Welwyn Control' and we find it being referred to at the Winsford accident in 1948.

I close on a bizarre note, or rather, notes. First odd item: many of the injured were found to be coated in a black grime, from some unknown source, which could not be removed in hospital even with ether. Second odd item: a Saturday night dance was in progress at the 'Cherry Tree' rooms nearby. When an appeal for cars was broadcast the dancers came pouring out, and the strange spectacle was witnessed of men and women in evening dress toiling among the rescuers. Lastly I must quote a remark by the stationmaster, justifiably proud of the promptitude with which aid was summoned. 'Never, I think,' he told a reporter, 'has there been a train smash with less confusion.'

CHAPTER 17

CASTLECARY
LONDON & NORTH EASTERN RAILWAY

We are in Scotland again, back in the murk of a snowbound winter twilight. The scene is the wayside station of Castlecary on the Edinburgh and Glasgow line of the former North British Railway, the date Friday, December 10, 1937, and the time, 4.37 p.m.

Since we encountered the North British at Elliot Junction, thirty-one years before, its accident record had been an unhappy one. There had been five serious accidents involving the deaths of twenty-two passengers all told, including a collision in 1917 at Ratho in which twelve passengers were killed. Castlecary overtopped them all. With its thirty-five dead it ranks only after the overwhelming catastrophes of Quintinshill and the Tay Bridge as the worst railway disaster in the history of Scotland.

The story of Castlecary is the history of a human failure to measure up to events. It is a drama complete with prologue and epilogue, and its theme is the behaviour of a rather strange individual under stress. Once again, as at Welwyn, the central figure is a signalman, but of a different sort from the miserable ineffective Shaw. Andrew, as I will call him, was well regarded by his superiors as a conscientious and reliable servant. He was, if I may use the term, something of a signal box lawyer; he had studied the rules to the point of obsession. A theorist rather than a practical signalman—despite his fifteen years' service—was the Inspecting Officer's verdict; emphatically not a man for a crisis. We shall see how this twist in his character, with the unwitting help of other parties, brought two trains to disaster.

It had been snowing all day at Castlecary, on and off. As darkness fell it was still snowing fairly thickly, in wet heavy flakes, reducing visibility to something under 500 yards. An east wind had driven the snow against the faces of the down line (Glasgow-bound) signals, rendering their lights almost invisible.

For the prologue we move to Gartshore, three block sections ahead in the Glasgow direction, where a pair of facing points had been put out of action by the snow. This happened about 4 o'clock, and it should have been a simple enough matter to clear them and get them working again. But two lengthmen bungled the job, as did the signalman also when he tried, and the down line was out of action for half-an-hour until a signal linesman could be fetched. By that time two trains were held up in rear, a passenger train at Croy and a goods at Dullatur East, the next station to Castlecary. Two Glasgow-bound expresses were due to follow, the 2 p.m. from Dundee and the 4.3 from Edinburgh. Signalman Smith at Dullatur had intended to clear a path for them by shunting the goods on to the up line, but this could not be done until two up passenger trains had passed.

The scene moves to the footplate of No. 9896 'Dandie Dinmont', a D29 4-4-0 at the head of the Dundee express, on a train of seven bogies with a fish van at the rear—the latter with a consignment that was to have gone by road, but was switched to the railway at the last moment. Driver Macaulay was peering out through the snow for a sight of the Castlecary distant signal. Even at 150 yards he could still not see the signal light, but against the last of the sunset he caught sight of the snow-whitened semaphore arm, standing—he was quite positive—at clear. He was travelling at about 55 m.p.h. and despite the weather was only two minutes behind time. He missed the home signal (which was at danger) because his attention was attracted by a red lamp being waved from the signal box. He braked on the instant, and brought his train to a standstill 468 yards beyond the box, the back of his tender level with the starting signal and the tail of his train not far beyond the platform end, 269 yards from the box. There was a track circuit behind the starter, on which the greater part of his train was standing. The time was 4.30.

I wrote in the last chapter about a test train being pulled up from 58 m.p.h. in 478 yards. It was from this test that the speed of Macaulay's train was deduced.

Having pulled up, Macaulay sent his fireman Fleming to the box to find out the cause of the stop. He failed to do one thing which might have made all the difference. He did not whistle to signify that he had stopped, though it is not certain whether the sound would have been heard in the box, against the wind and over a quarter of a mile away.

Let us now see what was happening in the box. The last down train—the goods—had passed at 4.9, and Andrew should have had Train Out of Section from Smith at Dullatur about 4.14. But though he did not receive it he made no inquiries, and though this had no bearing on the accident it shows his legalistic mind at work. Asked why he did not inquire what had happened to the goods, he replied that 'he was not in the habit of doing that for trains going to blocks in advance'. That was up to the man in the next box if he was in any doubt; he, Andrew, had done his part. However, he did ring at 4.22, after accepting the Dundee train from Greenhill Junction to the east, before offering the train forward. Then he learned that the goods was still held at Dullatur, and could not be shunted until the up passenger trains had passed.

As the Dundee train approached his box Andrew noticed that it had not reduced speed and was about to pass the home signal at danger. Hurriedly he waved a red light from the window and blew his whistle, but the train went by, as he imagined, still steaming. Andrew followed its course until the tail lamp was half-way along the platform, when a corner of the goods shed cut it off from his view. In his alarm he had not noticed that it was already slowing down to a standstill. He could have done one of two things. He could have gone to the window, from where he would have been able to see the tail light of the now stationary train. More simply, he could have looked at the track circuit indicator immediately in front of him, which was showing 'occupied'. Andrew did neither. He rushed to his instrument and sent the 4-5-5 Vehicles Running Away On Right Line signal to Dullatur, and followed it up with a phone call. 'He's run through my sticks,' he told Smith. He also sent for the station-master, Scott, who was at that moment returning from the Glenboig Fireclay Works which stands close to the station.

Having done this, Andrew bethought himself of the Edinburgh train, which had been offered from Greenhill Junction. As he was momentarily expecting word of a collision at Dullatur, it seems extraordinary that his mind should be occupied with accepting a following train. But bearing in mind what we know of his character, I think we can follow his train of thought. Where another man would have used his common sense and refused the train, Andrew asked himself what the rule-book said in such a situation. The 4.3

was an important train, he reasoned, and he must not hold it up unless there was a regulation which justified his doing so. In his self-induced perplexity he sought counsel of Signalman Beattie at Green-hill Junction : 'an older man than me, a man of very ripe experience'. Here is Beattie's account of the two calls which followed :

'On asking what was wrong, I was told that the goods was ahead standing at Dullatur East. I asked : 'Have you sent the Vehicles Running Away On Right Line signal?" He said : "I have done so." I also asked if he had put down detonators. He said : "No." "You should," I replied. He asked why, and I said : "It is always a precaution." This conversation took place at about 4.31. About a minute or two after he rang me again and asked : "Am I justified in clearing back the Dundee and taking on the 4.3?" I replied : "There is nothing to hinder you provided you saw the tail light and the regulations applied." I asked : "Are you certain all your signals are at danger?" He said : "Undoubtedly." I then asked : "Have you got your quarter mile clear ahead of your home signal? Are you certain of that?" He replied : "Yes." I then said : "There is nothing to prevent your accepting the 4.3." He then left the phone, cleared back the 2 o'clock ex Dundee, and accepted the 4.3 ex Edinburgh at 4.32.'

The fact that a collision at Dullatur would have held up the Edinburgh train in any case does not seem to have crossed Andrew's mind.

During the three minutes after 4.32 Andrew dealt with one of the passenger trains on the up line, and according to his own account he twice tried to phone Control, but the line was engaged both times. He also consulted the regulations with regard to the stopping of trains. He did nothing to try and find out whether or not the expected collision had occurred—that was the Dullatur man's business!

At 4.35 Fireman Fleming of the Dundee train reached the box. 'What is wrong?' he asked. 'Who are you?' asked Andrew, not recognizing him in the coat he was wearing. "I am the fireman of the passenger train," replied Fleming. 'Thank God you've stopped,' said Andrew, and went to the phone to tell Smith at Dullatur that the train had stopped in the section. Fleming corrected him. 'We are standing at the starting signal,' he said. But Andrew got the impression—or said he did—that Fleming had said : 'Through the signal'. Fleming signed the Train Register at 4.35, though the entry was afterwards clumsily altered to 4.38, by whose hand was never disclosed.

Fleming was followed into the box by Stationmaster Scott, who had seen the tail light of the Dundee train as he crossed the tracks on his way back from the fireclay works. But in the gloom, made thicker perhaps by the hanging smoke of the up train which had just passed, he over-estimated the distance and thought that the light was beyond the starting signal. That at least was his story. It is more likely that he did not look carefully, and gave himself—and Andrew —the benefit of the doubt in order to support the latter.

At 4.36 came the Train Entering Section signal from Greenhill Junction, a short 1¾-mile section. Andrew left the phone where he had been talking to Smith and turned to Fleming. 'I'll have to see about getting the 4 o'clock stopped,' he said. Exactly what, we may speculate, was in his mind? That to have stopped the train at the home signal, with the Dundee train less than 300 yards beyond, would have infringed the Quarter Mile Clear Ahead rule? Or did he wonder, after the way the Dundee train had disregarded the distant, whether that signal was really at caution? The question was never asked. He took up a hand lamp and some detonators and hurried out of the box, followed by Scott and Fleming. They had only time to fix one detonator properly when A3 Pacific No. 2744 'Grand Parade' at the head of the 4.3 came roaring out of the snowstorm, bearing down on them at a speed of nearly 70 m.p.h.

In charge of 'Grand Parade' was Driver Anderson. At forty-two he was young for an express driver, albeit only a spare one as yet. In his case too I think we may discern the workings of character. We recognize him as one of those keen drivers determined at all costs to keep time, the sort which is a godsend to the operating department. He had been 1½ minutes down at Polmont and was travelling rather faster than usual in order to get back on schedule. Too fast indeed for safety in such conditions. Rule 127 (iv) lays down:

'When owing to fog, falling snow or other cause the fixed signals are not visible at the usual distance, (the driver must) use every precaution and reduce speed if necessary.'

There could be no doubt that Anderson was stretching the rule in the interests of punctuality.

Like Macaulay eight minutes earlier, Anderson was peering out to catch sight of the Castlecary distant. It had grown that much darker, and he was travelling faster. He was something under 100 yards away when he managed to observe the arm, standing distinctly at clear. On that point he was as positive as Macaulay. As he passed the signal he looked back and caught a second glimpse of it by the light of the open fire door. He missed the home signal at danger, but saw the red hand lamp that Andrew held up to him from the lineside. 'This is something unusual," he remarked to his Fireman Kinnear, and moved to apply the brake. Then he heard the crack of the detonator and saw the tail light of the Dundee train ahead. He made a full brake application but could do little more than slightly check speed. 'Hold on,' he called out to Kinnear as he braced himself for the crash.

It was another Welwyn, only more so. The fish van at the rear of the Dundee train disintegrated, its providential last-minute attachment probably saving a few lives. The two coaches ahead of it were destroyed, and all seventeen passengers in them killed, as were five others in the next coach (the fifth)—a total of twenty-two out of the 110 passengers in the train. There was no telescoping; as Sir Nigel Gresley put it afterwards, the two rear coaches were simply squashed. The whole train was pushed forward fifty-two yards, and Driver Macaulay was badly injured.

'Grand Parade' for its part ploughed up seventy yards of track and came to rest on its side embedded in the embankment ninety-six yards from the point of collision. The bodies of the three leading coaches parted from their bogies, which piled up behind the tender and formed a ramp by means of which the first two coaches shot clean over the engine and landed upright beyond it athwart the tracks. The third coach came to rest twelve feet in the air, on top of the engine and tender. Considering that there were 200 passengers in the Edinburgh train, the number of dead was remarkably small; six in the leading coach and seven in the second.

The coaches of both trains were fitted with buckeye couplers and Pullman vestibules, which once again proved their worth. All the vehicles in the Edinburgh train behind the third remained in alignment, as did the first four vehicles of the Dundee train. The last three coaches of the Edinburgh train remained on the rails, and passengers stepped out of them on to the platform unaware that there had been a collision. As one lady wrote: 'I did not suffer from shock at all, as it only seemed to me as if the train had been pulled up badly.'

Fire played its part in the disaster, but in a kindlier role. Great bonfires made from the splintered woodwork lighted the rescuers in their task.

Anderson and Kinnear had remarkable escapes. The former was not injured at all; the latter after being trapped in the cab and reported killed was rescued with a slight wrist injury and a burn on his cheek, caused by acid dripping from the battery of the coach above.

Meanwhile Andrew was telephoning to Beattie to check the times of the Train Register entries. He told Beattie that he had 'got everything', meaning that he was clear of blame as far as the rules were concerned.

Much later, at about 6 o'clock, the injured Macaulay managed to drag himself to the box. He wanted to know the position of that distant. 'Have you a repeater on that distant?' he asked. 'No,' replied Andrew. 'You gave me a clear signal,' said Macaulay. At this Andrew exploded in righteous indignation. 'Oh, don't come that stuff,' he said. 'All right, there's no use getting angry about it,' replied Macaulay, and limped out of the box.

But no one ever discovered what the distant was showing, not even the Inspecting Officer, Lt.-Col. Mount, though he spent a great deal of time trying to find out. The inquiry ran into seven days, the evidence to 910 pages and the report to sixty-three pages—all of these records, surely. With the aid of models Macaulay reckoned that the arm of the distant had been inclined at 31 degrees from the horizontal. Anderson thought 37 degrees; the full off position was 48½ degrees. Andrew for his part affirmed that he could see the back light (showing arm at caution)—777 yards from his box—when he phoned Beattie just after 4.30, but the Inspector did not believe him. On the other hand there was no evidence to show that he had moved the lever after 4.9, when he had restored it after passing the goods train. That the distant should have been showing a true clear was ruled out by the fact that the home and starting signals were at danger. It was proved that weight of snow could not possibly have caused the arm to droop to anything like 30 degrees. The only explanation to fit all the evidence was that the arm had failed to return to normal when Andrew restored the lever at 4.9, and that was shown to be in the highest degree unlikely. Had both drivers been in error, or was the signal, for whatever reason, showing clear? Without actually expressing an opinion, the Inspector intimated that he preferred the drivers' evidence to Andrew's.

There was much less doubt about the position of the track circuit indicator, which Andrew had failed to notice when he thought that the Dundee train was running away. He maintained that he had looked at it afterwards and that it was showing clear when he phoned Beattie; the latter confirmed that Andrew had told him so. When after the accident the indicator showed 'occupied' Andrew tried to suggest that the Dundee train must have moved back, and when that explanation failed he fell back on the assertion that it must have been showing a false clear, for which he blamed the maintenance man, Robertson. His line of argument here gives us a further insight into his ways of thought. Robertson admitted having forged Andrew's signature on some of the time sheets, for what reason is not clear. Very well then, argued Andrew, he has been falsely claiming to maintain the circuit (which was not true), so what the indicator shows, correct or not, is his responsibility, not mine. But the Inspector was in no doubt as to what had happened. It was yet another case of a man thinking he saw what he expected to see. Andrew believed that the Dundee train had run through his signals, and that the indicator would therefore be showing clear. In this belief he was supported by the Stationmaster's wrong estimate of the distance of the tail lamp, whether genuine or (as the Inspector suspected) fabricated in order to cover Andrew. The circuit was tested afterwards and found to be in perfect working order.

The main feature of the case, as the Inspector pointed out, was Andrew's acceptance of the Edinburgh train two minutes after he had supposed the Dundee train was running away and was about to collide with the goods. It is difficult, wrote the Inspector, to believe that a responsible signalman could do such a thing, still less plead justification because block telegraph regulations do not prohibit such action in the circumstances which he alleged. But it was surprising that such an experienced signalman as Beattie should have acquiesced in the acceptance of the Edinburgh express.

Both drivers came in for criticism, though the Inspector's strictures were mild enough. He agreed that both had accepted the distant signal in good faith as clear. It would be unfair to criticize Anderson, he concluded, except for driving at a speed possibly in excess of that which was justified in the adverse weather conditions. Macaulay too might have infringed the spirit of Rule 127 (iv), while he might have prevented the accident if he had whistled.

Who then, if anybody, might have expected to find himself arraigned after the accident? Not Andrew. I said that this story had an epilogue, and it is a rather unpleasant one. It would seem that someone in authority demanded a scapegoat, and the choice of victim fell on Driver Anderson. If the Inspector's report had been available a charge could hardly have been brought, but where Court proceedings are involved the report is not published until after they are concluded. So it contains a footnote, which I quote verbatim:

'Before the Lord Justice-Clerk, in the High Court of Justiciary at Edinburgh, and a jury of nine women and six men, Driver D. J. Anderson was tried on a charge of culpable homicide on the 30th March. The Lord Advocate withdrew the charge on the 31st March, the jury was directed to return a verdict of "Not Guilty" and Driver Anderson was discharged.'

CHAPTER 18

NORTON FITZWARREN
GREAT WESTERN RAILWAY

Those who had to do much travelling in World War II will remember the nightmare of journeys in the blackout. The crowded trains, the dim lighting, the incessant delays, made train travelling, which should be a pleasure, into a hell. We had little thought to spare for the even harder lot of the railwaymen, short-staffed and handling a swollen traffic, and not least that of the enginemen, blinkered in their anti-glare screens and with many of their familiar landmarks invisible. It is remarkable that throughout the war we have only two really major disasters to record. Both took place during the blackout.

This accident brings us for the first and last time in this book to the Great Western Railway. That that Company had such a clear record was in no sense due to chance. If any of the pre-grouping Companies rightly deserved the title of Premier Line it was the Great Western. It had the greatest length of track, by far the best-designed locomotives, the fastest trains, and the longest non-stop run in the world. More to the point in the present connection, from 1906 it had developed its system of automatic train control (ATC), with audible warning to the driver, applied at the distant signal. This consisted of a ramp on the track not electrically energized when the signal was at caution, in which case a siren sounded in the cab and the brakes were partially applied. If the signal was at clear the ramp was energized and a bell sounded. It was this system which Inspecting Officers pleaded in vain, in one accident report after another, for other Companies to adopt.

So for half-a-century up to 1940 the Great Western had been practically free from serious accidents. The last grave one had been at Norton Fitzwarren in November 1890, when a broad gauge Cape Mail special had collided with a stationary goods train which had been shunted and forgotten by the signalman; ten lives were lost.

In the days before ATC, in 1900, there had been a mishap at Slough, where the driver overran a succession of signals at danger, while there had also been the derailment at Lougher Bridge which I mentioned in the account of the Sevenoaks accident, caused by the instability at speed of a saddle tank engine which was acting as pilot to an express. This accident incidentally gave rise to a Great Western operating peculiarity. Thereafter it was laid down that any assisting engine must be attached next to the train, so that the original train engine remained at the head.

But the long immunity could not last for ever. At 3.47 a.m. on November 4, 1940, on a pitch black morning at Norton Fitzwarren, fifty years almost to the day after the previous accident at the identical spot, the 9.50 night express from Paddington to the West of England ran through junction trap points on to open ground with the loss of twenty-seven lives.

The 9.50 was headed by 'King' class No. 6028 'King George VI' (originally 'King Henry II'), with a thirteen-coach train, jam-packed as usual with 900 passengers aboard. In charge was Driver Stacey, of Old Oak Common shed. It had left Paddington while the 'blitz' was actually on, which meant that it would have had a slow passage in the early stages. Travelling by the long route via Bristol it dragged its weary way into Taunton at 3.30 a.m., 1 hour and 8 minutes late. Meanwhile the 12.50 newspaper train, taking the direct route via Castle Cary (not to be confused with the Castlecary of our last accident), with a featherweight load of five vans and likewise hauled by a 'King', was running ahead of schedule. It was not due to stop at Taunton. Through Taunton from Creech St Michael to Norton Fitzwarren the line is four-track; the relief lines, added as recently as 1931, flank the main lines on either side. Signalman Wadham therefore, at Taunton West Station box, having learned from Athelney eight miles away that the newspaper train was still gaining time, decided to let it through on the fast line and dispatch the 9.50 on the relief—something which had seldom if ever been done before. The principal down platform at Taunton, at which the 9.50 had stopped, is actually on the relief line, which is nearest the station entrance, so it was a matter of sending the train forward on the same line instead of crossing it over again to the main line in the normal way.

Here we encounter yet another case of a railwayman seeing what he expected to see. Driver Stacey had been accustomed to see the down-relief-to-main line signal come off at the platform end; this time, of course, it was the down relief line signal which was off. He looked at it once, he said afterwards, and was quite certain that it was the relief-to-main-line signal which was off; he looked a second time and was equally certain, but a third time he was not so sure. However, he set off into the blackness all unaware that he was not on the main line as usual. As he passed the Taunton West Junction distant signal, on the same gantry as the Taunton Station West home, he thought he heard the ATC siren, though in fact he could not have done so. Between Taunton and Norton Fitzwarren the positioning of the signals is unusual. Normally Great Western signals are on the left, although the driver sits on the right. But when the relief lines were built sufficient distance was not left for the placing of signals between them and the main lines, so the main line signals were placed to the right, between the down and up tracks. Had these signals, at which Stacey was looking, been in the normal position, he would have seen that they were on his right instead of his left. As it was, they merely appeared a little further to the right than usual, not far enough for him to notice the difference. They were of course the signals for the newspaper train, now close behind, which Stacey was reading as his own. His own signals on the left he did not observe at all, because it did not occur to him to look that way.

So 'King George VI' gathered speed until according to the speedometer—all the 'King' class were so fitted—it was doing about forty as it approached Norton Fitzwarren. The convergence of the relief line with the main line is shortly beyond the station, and had this been showing lights as in peace time it would have provided Stacey with a clue. But in common with all other wayside stations is was blacked out for the duration.

We now come to the inexplicable part. The two Norton Fitzwarren distants—there was an additional inner one—were at caution, so as to slow the train for the junction with the main line. The ATC apparatus at the outer distant—found afterwards to be in perfect order—must therefore have given its siren-cum-brake warning, which Stacey must have cancelled. But he had no recollection of either the warning or the cancellation. Possibly this was the warning he thought he had heard on leaving Taunton, and he had got the time and place confused; at all events he did cancel it. Not for the first time, human fallibility had defeated the most elaborate safety devices. Only when the fellow 'King' on the newspaper train drew abreast in Norton Fitzwarren station did Stacey realize his mistake. It was then too late to avoid an accident; the junction catch-points lay only a hundred or so yards ahead. 'We are on the down relief,' he told his fireman, who was to die a few seconds later, and with that the engine went through the points and on to the soft ground beyond, coming to rest nearly fifty yards further on. There I saw it thirty-six hours later, as I travelled down to the West. We passed the scene of the accident at reduced speed, so that I was able to have a good look. 'King George VI' lay canted over on its left side, with its front end buried in the ground. It was carrying the bell presented to the first engine of the class, 'King George V', during its visit to America in 1927, a sad memento of happier days.

The Great Western did not use buckeye couplers, and the first five coaches were scattered over all four tracks. But the remainder kept the rails and were undamaged. Of the twenty-six passengers killed, thirteen were naval ratings; considering the crowded state of the train it is remarkable that casualties were not higher. The left-hand overturn of the engine, which killed the fireman, enabled Stacey to climb out of the cab uninjured.

Like a good railwayman, Stacey's first thought was to protect the line. In this waterlogged countryside he waded waist-deep back onto the tracks and made his way to Silk Mill Crossing box, a mile in the rear. There, agitated and dazed, he told the signalman that he was afraid he was responsible for the accident. At the inquiry the Inspecting Officer, Lt.-Col. Mount, dealt with him sympathetically. He was a top link driver with forty years' service, and the Inspector considered that his breakdown might be partly due to operating conditions in the blackout, also to the fact that his home at Acton had recently suffered air raid damage.

Well might the deathroll have been multiplied tenfold! For the end of the story is the tale of the most hairbreadth escape in the history of railway accidents. The enginemen of the newspaper train, behind their screens, were quite unaware that they were passing the express. So also was Guard Baggett, travelling in the fourth van. He was amazed when his window splintered and a metal object came hurtling through and struck him on the arm. Thinking there was something amiss with his train he applied the brake and brought it to a standstill at Victory Crossing, a mile further on. There he spoke with the driver, but as they could discover nothing wrong they decided to proceed cautiously to Wellington, where they learned of the accident.

The object which flew into the van was a rivet head from the bogie frame of 'King George VI'. Nor was that all. The panelling of the fifth van was scored with indentations made by the flying ballast as the express became derailed. The newspaper train had drawn clear in the nick of time. A second or two later and it would have ploughed into the packed carriages strewn across its path, to wreak a slaughter on the Quintinshill scale.

Even in disaster the Great Western's deserved good fortune had held.

CHAPTER 19

ECCLES

LONDON MIDLAND & SCOTTISH RAILWAY

'Come,' said the porter at Eccles, 'and I will show you.'

He led the way to the platform end and pointed to the retaining wall of the cutting just beyond. At a height of about a dozen feet the brickwork was broken and scarred. 'It took place just there,' he said. 'That's where the engine struck the cutting wall.' Thus has the Eccles disaster engraved its own memorial.

Eccles lies nearly four miles out of Manchester on the old Liverpool and Manchester line. Its most loyal citizen would hardly claim it as a beauty spot. It is part of that complex of towns known as the South-East Lancashire Conurbation, a region as unlovely as its name. The place seems made for fog and gloom, and it was in the fog-bound blackness of the morning of December 30, 1941, that two trains collided outside the station. A down train—from Manchester, that is—filled with workers ran sidelong into an up train, likewise full, as the latter was crossing from the slow to the fast lines. The time by the clocks was 8.18, but this was in the war, and though it was December Summer Time was in force. So it was still dark—thirty-seven minutes before the end of the blackout. Eccles is the second and last of our blackout accidents.

Here I must explain fog block working, which we shall meet again in the South Croydon accident in Chapter 22 and at Harrow in Chapter 25. Where there is a junction or conflicting train movements a train may in the normal way be allowed up to the junction home signal before being brought to a stop. It is thus allowed as far on its way as possible before being held up. But with traditional signalling an extra margin is called for in fog, and under fog block working the train would be held inside the signals of the previous box. (The procedure may vary somewhat from place to place, but that is the general principle.) Fog working at Eccles operated only in the absence of fogmen; once these were at their posts normal working could be resumed. I should add that it is exceptional to require fogmen at colour lights.

There were six fog posts at Eccles, but on this morning there were only three men available to man them. So these were allocated to the essential points which would enable fog block working to be suspended. The three fogmen rejoiced in the names of Parrington, Pantling and Patten. In the box at Eccles was a fairly new man, Signalman Lowe, and it is not surprising that he got the names mixed up.

The fog had been continuous for twenty-one hours, so that all three men had been out on duty the previous day for their full twelve-hour shift—the longest time allowed. The rule was that after this shift the fogman should have nine hours off—not an excessive rest period between two spells of such trying duty. In this case the fogmen had been withdrawn at 10 o'clock the previous evening so as to be on duty again at 7 a.m., ready for the heavy morning traffic. Or rather, two of them had been withdrawn then; for some reason Patten, at the down distants—fast and slow—had not been recalled until 11.30 p.m. So he was not due to resume until 8.30 a.m.

Fogmen going on duty had to report at the signal box either personally or by phone. Lowe expected Patten to phone and Pantling to report in person, or possibly he had already got the name confused. So when he heard a voice at 7 a.m. saying: 'I am going on duty now, Charlie,' he thought it was Pantling's. Whose voice it was remains a mystery, but it belonged to none of the fogmen. A minute or two afterwards Pantling phoned from the station, but Lowe thought it was Patten making his expected call. The booking boy, Acton, realized that it was Pantling, and so entered it in the register. He said afterwards that he had told Lowe he had done so, but Lowe either did not hear or mis-heard him, nor did it occur to Lowe to look in the register. Parrington had meanwhile reported and had gone to his post at the down outer home signals. 'I have all the fogmen on,' remarked Lowe to Acton. 'We are all right now.' With that he suspended fog working.

The fog was specially thick at Eccles—owing, it was said, to the proximity of the Manchester Ship Canal—and visibility was down in places to no more than ten yards. Because of the fog both trains were running late: the down train twenty-seven minutes late and the up train forty-nine. Many of the workers should by rights already have been at their jobs.

The up train, hauled by L.M.S. standard 2-6-2T No. 207 was being closely followed on the slow line by a train from Bolton, so it was decided to put it across at Eccles on to the fast line at the crossover at the Manchester end of the station. Exactly at that moment a down train was approaching on the slow line at about 30 m.p.h., having run past the distant and outer home signals at danger. Neither crew saw anything of the other train, though the fireman of the up train thought that he heard a swish as of a train passing. The next thing the crew of the up train knew was that they had been brought to a standstill by the breaking of the vacuum pipe. The down train, in the charge of 2-6-4T No. 2406, had struck the leading coach of the other train obliquely at the crossover. The locomotive tore through the carriages, completely destroying two and ripping off the sides of two others, finally coming to rest at an angle of 45 degrees against the cutting wall and making the marks which are still there to-day. The leading coach of the down train was also destroyed. In the two trains twenty-three persons lost their lives.

The collision had no sooner occurred than the uninjured passengers poured out of both trains. They made a huge bonfire of the wreckage, and set to work with a will to rescue the victims. 'There were hundreds of them at it,' said a railway inspector, 'you couldn't move for them.' The scene must have been rather like that at Ditton Junction nearly thirty years earlier, with an embarrassing superfluity of would-be helpers.

How had the down train come to collide with the other? If fog working had been in force it would have been held at the previous box, Cross Lane Junction. But as we have seen, Lowe had suspended working in the belief that Patten was at his post at the down distants, and so had accepted the train to the outer home, which meant that the distant had remained at caution. But the train had also run past the outer home, where Parrington was on duty. Why had it not been brought to a stop there? Here is the driver's story which he told at the inquiry.

After passing Cross Lane Junction (he said) he told his fireman to look out for the Eccles distant, which was on the latter's side. The fireman in evidence said the signal was showing green—possibly yet another instance of someone thinking he saw what he expected to see. Thus reassured by his fireman, and further reassured by the absence of a detonator, the driver accepted that the distant was at clear. He did not cross over the footplate to observe it himself, he explained, for fear that he might stumble on the way back, and so fail to be at the controls in time to stop at the outer home if necessary. He admitted, however, that though the fog post was on his side he had seen no one there.

At the outer home, the driver continued, he saw Parrington waving a green lamp. He described the lamp in detail: the flame was working up one side as if the wick were unevenly trimmed. He had heard no detonator.

Parrington contradicted this story absolutely. He had held up a red lamp, he said, and the detonator was in position and had exploded. On the latter point he was supported by one Bowden, the tail lamp man at Eccles box, who gave evidence that he had heard the detonator. The green light story was discounted by the fact that Parrington was standing on the far side of the fast lines, twenty-four yards from the train, and it was very doubtful whether in the dense fog the driver could have seen any lamp.

We have to conclude that the driver was lying, and embroidering his tale to make it sound convincing. The Inspecting Officer, Col. Wilson, evidently thought so, for he said bluntly that he believed Parrington. As to the detonator at the outer home signal, he gave the driver the benefit of the doubt. The engine was running chimney first, and it was possible that the sound had been muffled in the tank engine cab. But the driver should not have delegated the duty of observing the distant signal to his fireman, and he was not proceeding with the care necessary in a bad fog. However the Inspector put the main responsibility on Signalman Lowe. The latter had obviously got the names confused, but, said the Inspector, a glance at the register would have shown him his mistake. It was accepted, however, that his misconception about the fogman's duties was genuine.

At the inquiry the L.M.S. Railway announced that it was changing all distant signals on important routes to colour lights as they fell due for renewal, thus relieving railwaymen of one of their most disagreeable duties.

The accident, as I have said, took place at 8.18 a.m. At 8.30 a.m., prompt to time, Patten resumed duty.

CHAPTER 20

BOURNE END

LONDON MIDLAND & SCOTTISH RAILWAY

The fighting had stopped, but trains were still vast, slow and unpunctual. So it was with the night express from Perth, which came to grief on the fast-to-slow crossover at Bourne End, twenty-six miles from Euston, on the morning of September 30, 1945. It was the worst railway accident since Quintinshill thirty years before.

Crossover derailments have been comparatively rare in Britain. We have only noticed one so far; that was at Ditton Junction. There was another in 1931 at Leighton Buzzard, fourteen miles from Bourne End, in which four lives were lost. The driver of the Royal Scot class engine complained that his view of the signals had been obscured by steam blowing down on to the cab windows, a common fault with these engines in their unrebuilt state. As the classic and most disastrous of all, Bourne End stands by itself.

Of all the disasters recorded in this book Bourne End is in a sense the most inexplicable. More so even than Grantham; more than the appalling Harrow disaster to be described in Chapter 25. Grantham took place at night; at Harrow the driver had no foreknowledge that he was going to be checked. But at Bourne End a driver, forewarned by the working notices that he was to be diverted at this point, in clear daylight, disregarded two successive signal indications to reduce speed. He was a man, too, well known for his conscientious study of the notices. The Inspecting Officer thought that fatigue might have played its part, and this seems the only likely explanation.

Like Quintinshill, Bourne End was a case of death in the sunshine. It was a resplendent autumn morning without wind or cloud; one driver said the finest of the year. A low sun was shining almost into the eyes of the drivers of up trains, but that does not seem to have had anything to do with the accident.

It was a Sunday morning. The story begins at Crewe at 5 a.m., where rebuilt Royal Scot class 4-6-0 No. 6157 was waiting on the engine siding to take the Perth train forward. In charge was Driver Swaby, a man of fifty-five with sixteen years' driving experience. He was in the top link at Crewe and knew the London road intimately. He had volunteered for this turn, because it was hard to obtain top link drivers willing to undertake Sunday duty. This had happened, in fact, on four successive Sundays. There was no question of his having been under pressure; on the contrary, when Parker, the loco-motive platform regulator, came on to the footplate Swaby told him how pleased he was to have been given this particular job. He said moreover that if Camden shed were short of men for the Sunday evening turns he would be prepared to book off there, instead of returning 'on the cushions', and cover a job back to Crewe. His fireman, Jones, was prepared to do anything his mate did. But note that Swaby had booked on at 1.13 a.m.; he had already been at work for half the night preparing his own and another engine. Take that with what we learned at Shrewsbury about drowsiness on the footplate, and perhaps we have the clue to the disaster.

Swaby and Jones were having a long wait. The Perth express, clinging to its wartime habit, was running eighty minutes late. Swaby was filling in the time, Parker noticed, by reading the Fortnightly Notices by the light from the open firebox door. He made a habit of studying these carefully; as Parker told the inquiry: 'He was the very best man at Crewe for reading the notices. I have heard drivers go to him and ask him if there are any permanent way slacks.'

The page Swaby was reading was headed: 'Rugby–London', and among the Sunday diversions listed was the following item:

Date	Locality	Lines Affected	Particulars of Work and Instructions
Sunday, Sept. 30	Between Boxmoor and Watford, 23 and 18¼ m.p.	Up and Down Fast	7.0 a.m. to 5.0 p.m. Unloading new sleep-ers and loading rails and repairs to brick-work in Watford tunnel. BLOCKED (except for ballast trains). All trains to travel over the Slow Lines between Bourne End and Watford No. 1.

So Swaby had digested his warning.

The express left Crewe at 5.45, eighty-two minutes late. It consisted of fifteen vehicles, 328 yards long, well filled but not overcrowded with 398 passengers.

Our next news of Swaby is at Berkhampstead a minute or two after 9 o'clock. The express had been further delayed and was now running two hours late, but Swaby had managed to pick up a minute or two from Bletchley by a fast climb up to Tring—sure hallmark of a good driver. He was now running at 60 m.p.h. or so—about the highest speed normal under wartime conditions—down the long descent to London. The Berkhampstead signalman caught sight of Swaby and Jones—strange parallel with Grantham—and noticed that each was in his place, Swaby sitting down.

I must now describe the signalling at Bourne End, which was a half-way box between Berkhampstead and Hemel Hempstead (or Boxmoor as it was then called), 1¾ miles from each. The distant signals were colour lights; that for the fast line had three aspects: green, one yellow (outer home signal at danger) and two yellows—diversion to the slow line. It may be noted that elsewhere, with continuous colour lights, the double yellow has a different meaning, namely: the next light is showing a single yellow and the one beyond that red. The Bourne End outer home signal was a single upper quadrant arm, while the inner home consisted of splitting signals for the junction. The driver thus had two separate warnings of a diversion: at the distant and at the inner home.

At this time in the morning—8 o'clock Greenwich time—the sun was only 17° above the horizon, swinging about 10° from side to side as the line curved, thus coming momentarily directly in the driver's face. Every car driver knows how trying that can be, but the evidence of other drivers suggested that it could not have caused Swaby to miss or mis-read the signals.

Let us try to gauge the degree of Swaby's lapse from watchfulness. The distant with its double yellow came into view 590 yards beforehand; at 60 m.p.h. equal to about 20 seconds' travelling. For 1,175 yards after that, say 40 seconds, there would be no warning sign, for the outer home, as I have said, consisted of a single arm. Then the inner home showing the diversion came into view with 851 yards still to go before the crossover points—a further 30 seconds' travelling. If within the first 15 or even 20 seconds of this period Swaby had taken action to reduce speed he could have negotiated the crossover, for although there was a 20 m.p.h. limit it was estimated that it could be taken safely at up to 40. In fact it would seem he did nothing until he was actually on the crossover, or practically so; only about that point, if at all, were the brakes applied, while the regulator was found still open. Nor did Swaby blow his whistle. So for two separate periods of 20 and 30 seconds his mind, tragically, had been elsewhere than on his job. There could be no question of his having had trouble with the engine, which was in first-class condition.

Once again we can picture the moment on the footplate when the engine struck the crossover; the sudden terrible realization of catastrophe and the frantic too-late application of the brake. It was over quickly for Swaby and Jones, both of whom were killed instantly.

No. 6157 rolled to the right as it was deflected leftwards. It recovered and lurched heavily to the left, pushing the rails out of position in front of it. It reached the slow line still travelling at fully 50 m.p.h., continued for a short distance and then turned over to the left. On both sides of this point the line is in cutting, but just here, by unhappy chance, a short embankment intervenes. The engine dropped into a field nine feet below and slid on its side for over twenty yards, dragging six of the first seven coaches after it. They piled up into a vast heap of wreckage rising thirty feet above the engine. Perversely the second vehicle, an all-steel van, stayed on the top and was thrown on its side across three tracks, little damaged. Only the last three coaches kept the rails undamaged. It is a strange thought that while the engine was already plunging over the embankment the last seven coaches had not yet reached the crossover.

Including the driver and fireman, forty-three people died in this disaster, of whom five died later in hospital. The list of the seriously injured was exceptionally high; sixty-four were in hospital for over a week. Among the dead were five dining-car attendants from the Royal train who were returning home as passengers.

Apart from the signalman at Bourne End, who saw it all happen right in front of him (and was lucky not to have had his box swept away), there was one other witness to the accident. This was an American airman, Captain McCallum, who was taking off from Bovingdon airfield for Paris. When he saw the train overturn he radioed back for help, which was quickly forthcoming with typical American efficiency. Among other help the airfield sent heavy crane lorries, which proved invaluable in starting to clear the wreckage before the railway breakdown gangs arrived. When supplies of bandages for the injured ran out, the Americans replenished them. Thus, nearly forty years after Salisbury, the United States was again involved in a British railway accident; as I have said, in a very different role from then.

No. 6157 remained in its field for a month. Re-railing it was a major operation. It was not severely damaged, and after repair was put back to work.

The Inspecting Officer, Lt.-Col. Sir Alan Mount, concluded that it was useless to speculate on the causes of Swaby's lapse. But he did comment on the fact that the driver had done twenty-six days' continuous duty, including four Sundays. 'The action of certain men', he wrote, 'in not making themselves available for rostered and agreed service on Sundays must have resulted in greater strain being borne by others.' Beyond that, there was nothing more to say.

The Inspector had plenty to say about other matters. Once again he urged the need for some form of automatic train control. This recommendation had become standard form in cases where drivers had disregarded the signals, but on this occasion the Inspector was more insistent. 'It is all too easy', he wrote, 'to state a case against it on the basis that perfection and completeness are difficult of attainment; but that policy may, through fear of doing the wrong thing, lead to delay in the installation of any form of equipment.'

But it needed an even more terrible disaster before the railway management was at last galvanized into action. We shall come to that in due course. Meanwhile the Great Western with its ATC continued on its accident-free way.

An odd sidelight in the report concerned the duties of the guard. To me at least it goes far to explain why 'working to rule' has become an act of hostility to the travelling public. At the time of the collision Guard Horwood was in the thirteenth coach having a cup of tea with a sleeping-car attendant. Though the coach was not even derailed, both men were badly shaken and bruised. Now Rule 2 (i) reads:

'2. Employees MUST—
(i) see that the safety of the public is their chief care under all circumstances.'

According to that, and the specific rule for guards, Horwood should have been in his van, watching out for the diversion and ready to apply the brake in case the driver should fail to do so. He told the

Inspector, reasonably enough, that he had full trust in the driver. A guard has many duties, and he could never perform them if, in a 1,000-foot train, he had to get back to his van and keep a lookout at every point where the driver might fail to reduce speed. The Inspector appeared rather taken aback to find that the Company regarded the lookout rule as applying only at station stops, and he suggested that it should be stiffened specifically to cover diversions. But we begin to see why, if the railway employees decide to interpret every rule literally, the entire time-table seizes up. To make railway operation practicable at all the final arbiter must be common sense. But it may not look that way at an official inquiry, with the Inspecting Officer's stern eye on the witness.

The accident spotlighted a signalling point: the means used to warn a driver to slow down for a diversion. With semaphore signals the warning would have been given by splitting distants, repeated at the home or inner home signal. But where a colour light distant was used, the L.M.S. used the double yellow aspect for the purpose. With continuous colour lights, as has been explained, the double yellow meant something different—a single yellow at the next light—and it was suggested by one witness at the inquiry, though improbably, that Swaby might have been momentarily confused.

The Inspector suggested that the double yellow indication should be standardized to mean one thing only: one yellow at the next light. If used in conjunction with semaphore signals it should therefore be as an outer distant, with an inner distant showing a single yellow. As to the position of stop signals, clearance should be retarded in the case of a slow-speed diversion on a fast route to bring the speed down to safety level. This point was put to the Railway Clearing House, which took it time over a reply. This was not indeed published until after the Goswick accident (described in Chapter 23) more than two years later, when the same question arose in a different form. The reply appears in the report on that accident, but to complete the story I give it here:

'While the principle . . . could be adopted in certain cases, it could not be universally applied without detriment to the operation of the railways, having regard to the working of heavy freight trains and the incidence of gradients.'

The difficulty is one which applies much less to diesel or electric working—another bonus from the disappearance of steam—and the increased use of continuous colour lights on main lines will tend to eliminate the problem. How simple the diversionary process then becomes I observed for myself at Reading only the other day, when we were put across on to the slow lines outside the station. When our 'Western' diesel had been brought practically to a standstill at the red the diversionary 'feathers' appeared and the light changed to yellow. We picked up speed quickly as we ran into the platform. The loss of time—with a diesel—was minimal, and absolute safety was assured. Short of the driver cancelling his ATC warning, a Bourne End-type accident was impossible.

The site of the accident wants searching for now. It took a several miles' tramp along Hertfordshire lanes and a little discreet trespassing before I managed to locate it. For Bourne End has been wiped off the railway map. Signal box, crossovers, signals—all have gone; the continuous colour lights, controlled from Watford, wink beneath the catenary. A new crossover has been laid in 1½ miles away near Hemel Hempstead, and there is not even a trace to mark the site of the box. The field into which No. 6157 plunged was carrying a rather sickly-looking crop of barley. But I will give a clue as to how to recognize the spot. Look out for mile post 26, which is on the down side. Then cross over the carriage quickly, and there is a brief dip in the ground which breaks the cutting. That is where No. 6157 fell over, dragging nearly half her train with her, on a brilliant Sunday morning in autumn.

CHAPTER 21

LICHFIELD

LONDON MIDLAND & SCOTTISH RAILWAY

The collision at Lichfield on the evening of New Year's Day 1946 falls in the rare class of unique accidents. We have only had one genuinely unique one so far; that was at Weedon, and this one at Lichfield is the only other. Hull Paragon was indeed unique in its unlikelihood, but it belongs to the general category of signalman's errors. At Lichfield a handful of frozen ballast interfered with the working of a set of points. Although other factors were involved, it was the movement of the ballast which precipitated the accident.

Lichfield was remarkable for another reason, though one which in the story of accidents is by no means unique. Time and again we have had to record how a railwayman has managed to mis-see something. Sometimes, like the driver at Eccles, he may have been lying to cover up his negligence, but more often one feels that the mistake was due to genuine self-deception. So far the men concerned have been interested parties, who may unconsciously have bent the facts in their own favour. But at Lichfield three quite independent witnesses—not involved in the accident in any way—were prepared to testify that red was green. Interrogated separately four times by three different sets of people, they stuck to their story. That is a circumstance without parallel.

A short description first of the scene. The platforms at Lichfield Trent Valley station stand on the slow lines, which flank the fast lines for about 600 yards to the north of the station and through it, converging again at the south end of the platforms. In the southbound direction there are two connections from the fast to the slow lines: the first where the up slow line commences, controlled by Lichfield No. 2 box, and the other about 400 yards beyond, near the north end of the up platform, controlled by No. 1 box. To complete the picture: just by the No. 1 box connection a spur runs from the up slow line to the Walsall–Burton line, which crosses over the main line at right angles.

Let us take a closer look at the No. 1 box connection. This was controlled by levers No. 33 (facing) and No. 34 (trailing), together with No. 32, which actuated the locking bolt for No. 33. Since this bolt played a key part in the accident I had better explain its function. All facing points must be locked in position, which is done by means of a bolt which engages in a notch in the stretcher joining the two tongues of the points. The bolt is worked by a separate lever, which when pulled engages it in the notch. This lever is normally kept in the reversed position. When the points are to be moved it must be restored to normal in order to free them, after which it is reversed again to restore the lock.

January 1st was a fine clear evening with a few degrees of frost. The 6.8 p.m. slow train from Stafford to Nuneaton, a short four-coach train hauled by Prince of Wales class 4-6-0 No. 25802, had run into Lichfield station at 6.52 over the No. 1 box connection. Normally the other connection was used, but the slow line between the two was occupied by a goods train waiting to go forward along the Burton spur.

Close behind the slow was the 2.50 p.m. express fish train from Fleetwood to Broad Street, another short train of seven fish vans and a brake van hauled by Stanier Class 5 4-6-0 No. 5495. It was due to pass the slow train at Lichfield, and had been on the other's heels ever since Stafford, suffering check after check.

At 6.46 Signalman Williams in No. 1 box had set the points for the local. At 6.52, having sent Train Out Of Section to No. 2 box, he re-set the road for the fish train. At least he thought he had done so. But in those six minutes the ballast had moved, whether forced up by the frost or by the movement of trains, or both. I need not go into technicalities, but the effect was to impede the movement of the locking bolt mechanism, so that as Williams restored No. 32 locking bolt lever to normal the bolt was not quite free of the notch. He then restored lever 33 to normal for the fish train, but the points were still held locked by the bolt. So though the lever moved the points did not, i.e. they were still set for the connection to the slow line. It may seem extraordinary that the lever could thus be moved against the resistance of the rodding, but without knowing it Williams had bent the vertical down rod leading from the lever to the rodding on the ground. The rest of the movement had been taken up by the springing in the rod-ding. Although Williams was a small man weighing only 9½ stone, the movement had required no special effort which might have warned him that something was wrong.

The return of lever 33 to normal freed the interlocking, and Williams was able to pull off his signals for the fish train. The signal that matters is the home signal, lever No. 4, which protected the connection. On the same gantry was signal No. 6, fast to slow, also a rarely-used signal No. 7, fast to Burton spur. Williams pulled No. 4 with the other fast line signals, and assumed that it was off. He thought he had looked to make sure that the back light was obscured as it should have been, but was not certain of this. In any case he had no cause to doubt that the signal had been correctly pulled. In fact it had not been pulled off. The points, as we have seen, had remained set for the connection, and there is a device known as a detector, an additional safeguard to interlocking, provided against this very con-tingency. It prevents a signal being pulled off in conflict with the setting of the points. Since the detector was found afterwards to be in perfect order there could be no doubt that No. 4 had remained at danger; when Williams had pulled the lever he had merely stretched the wire. But he was now free to pull off both distants, outer and inner.

Driver Read of the fish train, tired of the incessant delays, wel-comed the sight of the outer distant colour light at green. 'We are going to get a clear road at last,' he remarked to his fireman Beckett. The inner distant was also at clear, and so, Read confidently affirmed afterwards, was the home signal—No. 4. He told the inquiry he was quite certain that it was the right hand of the three signals which was at clear. The next moment the engine gave a violent lurch as it was deflected over the connection, throwing Read into the middle of the cab. He had no idea what had happened, but had the presence of mind to shut off steam and apply the brake before striking the rear of the stationary slow train. Thinking back to the Bourne End accident, it is interesting to note that Read's engine had traversed a very similar crossover at 35–40 m.p.h. without being derailed.

The slow train was standing with the brakes on, but none the less it was driven forward for nearly 100 yards, the engine ending up in the sand drag at the end of the slow line. The three last coaches of the train were wrecked and the leading coach driven into the tender and badly damaged. The fish train came to rest some 130 yards beyond the point of impact. No. 5495 had driven right through the rearmost coach, whose roof and body sides were found abreast of the tender, with the sole bars splayed out on either side of the engine. Half the second coach was found on the station platform. Thirteen passengers were killed outright and another seven died in hospital or on the way, a total of twenty, while twenty-one were injured. Few can have escaped unharmed. None of the enginemen suffered serious injury, though Driver Read had to be taken to hospital with severe shock. Luckiest escape was that of the slow train guard, who was having a cup of tea in the buffet.

After the accident Fireman Beckett of the fish train came into the box. A highly mystified Williams, who took him for the driver, assured him that all the signals had been cleared for his train. The guard of the fish train, Freeman, also came into the box, and was likewise assured.

As I have said, it was not only Driver Read who was convinced that No. 4 signal was at clear. The three independent witnesses who supported him were the driver and guard of the waiting goods train and the signalman in No. 2 box, all of whom were well placed to see the signal. Here are the stories they told to the Inspecting Officer, Lt.-Col. Woodhouse.

Driver Kendall, of the Burton goods, had been waiting for nearly an hour just forward of the home signals. He had glanced back from time to time to see if his own signal, No. 12, had cleared for his train to start. He could see the back lights of the signals plainly, also the outline of the signals themselves against the night sky. He noticed No. 6 signal being cleared for the slow train and returned to danger behind it, as this meant that there was nothing now to prevent his own train leaving. Shortly afterwards he saw No. 4 signal move to clear, about three minutes before the fish train arrived. He had remarked on this to his fireman Harley: 'They've pulled off for the main again, they're busy tonight.' After the accident Harley went to the station, where he saw Guard Freeman of the fish train. It was arranged that Harley should go back to No. 2 box to protect the obstruction.

Guard Moors of the goods train was equally definite. He could see the home signals clearly from his seat through the front windows of his van, and he glanced at them from time to time through force of habit. He remembered the arrival of the slow train, on which he sometimes worked. He thought he saw all the signals at danger after the train had passed, but it might have been before. When he heard the fish train coming he looked again. It was only a casual glance, but he was sure that No. 4 was then at clear; it had gone back to danger when he next looked at it, after the accident. Not long afterwards he saw Driver Kendall and learned that he also had seen No. 4 at clear.

The third witness was Signalman Shone in No. 2 box. After pulling his own distant signal lever, which with No. 1 box jointly controlled the colour light, he had looked at the No. 1 box home signals, as was his custom from time to time, and saw that No. 4 was at clear. Though this was no more than a glance he was quite sure he was not mistaken. He knew the pattern of signals on the gantry well, and if it had been No. 6 signal, for example, showing green, he would have remembered it. On hearing the noise of the collision he went to the door of his box, and thought No. 4 signal was still at clear. He did not learn what had happened until an hour later, when Williams telephoned him.

It was established that none of these three could have had any conversation with Driver Read, who had been taken to hospital directly after the accident. They had been questioned, separately, a few hours after the accident, then again at the Company's inquiry, then twice by the Inspecting Officer, and their accounts were the same in each case.

Here was a poser for the Inspecting Officer, faced, as he put it, with this incompatibility between the oral and the tangible evidence. However having exhausted every possibility he was forced to the conclusion that No. 4 signal could not have been at clear. Driver Read's mistake—as it must have been—was understandable. Having had a succession of checks he welcomed the green colour light, confirmed by the green inner distant, and assumed he had a clear road ahead. He probably missed the home signal looking out for the starting signal beyond No. 1 box, and imagined afterwards that he had seen it showing green. But what of the independent witnesses?

Here was Col. Woodhouse's explanation. It is rather a mouthful of a sentence, but I must quote it in full. He wrote:

'There is always a likelihood of auto-suggestion in the light of afterknowledge when an endeavour is made to recall subsequently the precise details or sequence of incidents so familiar as to call for no special notice at the time of their occurrence.'

What had happened, the Inspector thought, was this. Williams had told Beckett, the fireman of the fish train, that all the signals on the up fast line had been cleared. That started a chain of suggestion. Beckett, it was discovered, had passed the information to Guard Freeman, who had also heard it from Williams himself. Freeman had then gone to the station and seen Harley, the fireman of the goods train, to whom he passed on the information. Harley passed it on to his driver Kendall, who in turn passed it on to Guard Moors. As for the man in No. 2 box, Shone, Williams when he phoned would undoubtedly have told him that everything had been in order. None of these witnesses had any special interest in the position of the signals. Several trains had passed on the up fast line during the previous hour, so all three had seen No. 4 signal at clear more than once. When they were told that it had been at clear for the fish train, this caused them to relate the information to what they had seen earlier, with identical inaccurate results.

As I said in the first chapter, a study of railway accidents is an education in the human capacity for self-deception. The Lichfield accident is surely the classic example.

Since it may be accepted that Read passed No. 4 signal at danger it might be claimed that the reversed points were not the cause of the accident. It is also true that Signalman Williams ought to have noticed that the back light was still showing, as it must have been. To that extent both men had a degree of responsibility. It remains true that the accident would not have happened if the ballast had not blocked the locking bolt mechanism, a circumstance that remains unique.

CHAPTER 22

SOUTH CROYDON
SOUTHERN RAILWAY

The last months of independent railways in Britain, before they were swept into the maw of British Railways, were marked by two serious accidents at opposite ends of the country, which occurred within two days of each other. The first took place at South Croydon Junction, where the line from Oxted joins the Brighton main line, on the morning of October 24, 1947. One electric train ran into the rear of another as the latter was gathering speed from a check; it is our second and last all-electric accident.

So far we have had no accidents to record in the London area. There have indeed been several on the outer periphery—Sevenoaks, Welwyn, Bourne End—but London proper, the area now controlled by the Greater London Council, has escaped our purview. That has been due to good luck rather than to any special immunity attaching to capital cities. Paris, for example, has experienced the most horrible of all kinds of accident—fire in a tunnel; that was on the Metro in 1903, when eighty-four persons were killed. At Christmastide 1933 there was a Quintinshill-scale collision on the C.F. de l'Est at Pomponne, 16 miles out of Paris, when 220 were killed. This accident, which occurred in thick fog, was caused by a danger-side failure of the ATC apparatus. London has indeed had its share of what one might call second-degree accidents. The Metropolitan, after forty years of steam operation without killing a passenger, had its first fatal accident at West Hampstead in 1907, when one electric train ran into the rear of another. Three passengers were killed. On January 1, 1915 a sidelong collision, rather similar to the one at Eccles, took place on the Great Eastern at Ilford between a local train and an up Clacton express, killing ten people. There was the same death-roll at Battersea Park on the Southern in 1937, when a Victoria-bound electric collided with a stationary steam train. Two further bad accidents took place on the Great Eastern line, one at Ilford in January 1944, when a train ran past three colour lights in fog, killing four people, and a collision at Gidea Park in January 1947, when seven were killed.

None of these however produced that grim characteristic of metropolitan accidents—a huge death-roll. As has been pointed out, the number of killed in a given accident hinges to a great extent on the number of people in the train or trains, and if a crowded suburban train is involved the chances are that the casualty list will be heavy. So it proved to be when the law of averages at last took effect and London had a run of major disasters; three in the ten years 1947–1957. All took place in the rush hours, and in two of them fog took a hand. Considering how much London suffers from fog each winter it is surprising that nothing on such a scale had happened before. The first of the series, and the least calamitous in loss of life, was the one at South Croydon.

The morning had dawned misty in south London, and the fog thickened rapidly until by half-past eight visibility was down to 50 yards or less. In the box at Purley Oaks was a young man named Hillier, a porter returned to railway service after three years as a prisoner of war, who had trained as a signalman only six months before, and whose experience of the box was limited to nine full weeks and some odd turns. Since it had been summer time, he had had no experience of the box in fog. He is in all probability alive today, so let me say at once that though he blundered—and how many of us do not at times?—there is nothing in the record in any way to his discredit as a person. However tragic the results of his mistake, it arose from a commendable desire not to delay the rush-hour traffic. I see no reason therefore why I should not mention his name.

There are two stations, Purley Oaks and Purley, within a mile of each other. The signal box at the north end of Purley station is known as Purley North. The box at Purley Oaks stood 170 yards beyond the south end of the station. It was a small box with only thirteen levers in use, but an extremely busy one. In the course of a single hour in the peak period 38 trains were booked to pass on the four tracks, for each of which three levers had to be pulled and returned. That meant 228 lever movements—nearly four a minute—as well as 90 to 100 bells and plunging (as we shall see in a moment) for each train. The stress of such intensive traffic in first-time-ever fog conditions provided exactly the circumstances to cause a lapse by an inexperienced man. In fact, he should not have been in such a busy box at that stage of his experience. The Inspecting Officer said so, and so did Hillier's colleague Neary at Purley North. He should have been allowed to graduate through a lower-grade box. As Neary put it: 'It did seem unfair to put a porter-signalman with a few weeks' experience out on the main line.'

In Signalman Neary, a man with thirty-eight years' service, we have a glimpse of a sterling and capable personality. The contrast between the experienced and considerate old hand and the anxious novice provides one of those character studies which form such a fascinating sidelight to these stories.

The Brighton main line at this time was operated on the Sykes lock-and-block system, the invention of a Victorian engineer of that name. The Southern Company had decided before the war to instal track-circuiting and colour lights, but this like all other such developments had been brought to a halt. The basic principle of the Sykes system is the same as that of the Tyers single line system which we encountered at Abermule, namely, that signal movements can only take place with the co-operation of the man at the other end of the block. To explain briefly: in the case of boxes at A, B and C, the signalman at A can lower his most advanced signal when it is freed by the man at B operating a plunger on his instrument. When B pulls his home signal, a tablet on the instrument normally showing 'free' changes to 'locked'. B in turn can only lower his starting signal when C has plunged on his instrument. B's instrument meanwhile remains locked. Ahead of the starting signal is a treadle operated by the train, which must be depressed by the train passing over it before the starting signal can be replaced. This signal likewise has its instrument, which normally shows 'locked' but changes to 'free' when the treadle is operated, and returns to 'locked' when the signal is replaced. Only when this has taken place does the home signal instrument also again show 'free', and only then can B plunge again to release box A's starter. Thus B cannot accept a second train from A until the previous one has passed beyond his starting signal. That is not the whole of the system, but it is enough for our purpose.

Naturally provision must be made to interrupt the normal sequence if necessary. A train accepted, for example, may be cancelled. So a key is provided to enable the instrument to be re-set. It is important to ensure that the key is not put to the wrong use—to do so, in fact, in the Southern Railway's instructions, was to incur the danger of dismissal. Hillier's instructor's advice was to 'treat it as a red-hot poker and handle it as such'. The instructor, I may say, had commented favourably on Hillier's steady manner.

Here we again encounter fog working at South Croydon Junction, the box on the London side of Purley Oaks. Trains in clear weather were accepted up to the Up Main signal, only 276 yards in rear of the junction, when a train had been accepted from the Oxted line. But in fog trains were held in Purley Oaks station, behind the starting signal. Unlike the system at Eccles, the arrangement operated even when the fogmen were out, as they were on this morning.

Please note the two vital signals at Purley Oaks; the home signal, lever No. 18, close to the box, with the instrument on which the signalman plunged to release the starting signal at Purley North, and the starting signal No. 19 at the north end of the station, similarly controlled by the instrument at South Croydon Junction. Note also that up trains were belled on the 3 pause 1 signal, except trains from the Tattenham Corner-cum-Caterham branches, which join the main line at Purley station and were belled 3 pause 3 pause 1.

The time was 8.23. Neary at Purley North offered the 7.33 from Haywards Heath to Hillier, who accepted it at once. Neary sent the Train Entering Section signal at 8.27 and expected to receive Out Of Section a minute or two later—the boxes were only 1,280 yards apart. But no signal came. In the meantime the 8.4 from Tattenham Corner had arrived at Purley station and had had its Caterham portion attached, while on the main line at 8.33 a train from Ore had been announced from Coulsdon South. Neary had to decide which of the two to accept, so he picked up the phone to Hillier. He might have asked straight out why he had received no Out Of Section signal, but as he explained at the inquiry; he wanted to avoid making Hillier feel 'uncomfortable by saying anything about delaying the Out Of Section signal, as this would have been inclined to put the man off his balance.' He added that he had 'never worked with a better porter-signalman'. So he simply asked in a friendly way: 'How he was looking on the Up Main'. The only answer he received was 'Gor Blimey', and the receiver was replaced. Neary could make nothing of this, but a few seconds later he received from Hillier the Out Of Section signal. He decided to send forward the Tattenham Corner train, which he offered on the 3-3-1 code. Hillier accepted it correctly.

The Haywards Heath train had been standing for some minutes at Purley, and every commuter knows what happens then. Passengers arriving for the next train crowd into the one they see waiting. The train left Purley with something like 1,000 passengers in a nine-coach train seating 750.

Let us see what had been happening at Purley Oaks. At 8.26½ Hillier offered the Haywards Heath train to South Croydon Junction, but Signalman Walder there decided not to accept it but to give preference to an Oxted line train which was next in the booked order. So starting signal No. 19 remained locked. In clear weather the train could have gone forward to the Junction home signal, but in fog working, as I have explained, it was held at Purley Oaks station. It was invisible from the box in the fog, and in the pressure of work Hillier forgot all about it. A steam engine might have given some audible reminder of its presence by blowing off and so forth, but electrics are silent both at rest and starting. Meanwhile the same scene was being enacted in Purley Oaks station as at Purley. Arriving travellers were piling into the standing train, which when it left had 800 passengers in its eight coaches seating 536.

Hillier was still waiting for Walder's acceptance when Neary made his enquiry. Hillier glanced at his No. 18 instrument and saw that it showed 'locked', as it was bound to do with a train still in the section. With that train forgotten and invisible, we can understand the moment of panic which prompted his 'Gor Blimey' to Neary. Good Lord, have I been holding up the traffic? Why is the instrument showing 'locked' when the line is clear? It must have failed. (There had been previous failures which encouraged him in this belief). The rules said that in such a case he should consult the signalman on either side, but he did not think to do so. It is clear, I think, that he was pre-occupied with not causing delays to the exclusion of everything else. Without further ado he used the key and re-set the instrument. He then hastily gave Neary Out Of Section, accepted the Tattenham Corner train on the 3-3-1 code and pulled off his home signal.

Just afterwards South Croydon Junction accepted the Haywards Heath train on the 3-1 code and plunged, thus freeing starting signal 19. Hillier supposed that the acceptance was for the Tattenham Corner train, which he had not offered, though he might have noticed from the bell signal that it was not. As the Haywards Heath train silently left the station it operated the treadle beyond signal 19 and changed that signal's instrument from 'locked' to 'free'. Mystified, Hillier assumed another false indication and re-set this instrument too without moving the lever, which was still pulled off behind the Haywards Heath train. Thus the Tattenham Corner train, which was not due to stop at Purley Oaks, passed under clear signals.

Walder at the Junction had pulled off his home signal for the Haywards Heath train, but could not clear his distant for two or three minutes until South Croydon Station box, which controlled it, had cleared the Oxted line train ahead. So the Haywards Heath train was slowed down at the distant to about 15 m.p.h. It was picking up speed again when the Tattenham Corner train, travelling at 40-45 m.p.h., crashed into its rear.

Surprisingly, serious damage was confined to the two vehicles actually colliding, but these were almost totally wrecked. The leading buffers of the Tattenham Corner train underrode the rear ones of the Haywards Heath train, and the body of the leading coach was swept away, save for the last two compartments. Most of the casualties occurred in this coach. The rear coach of the Haywards Heath train was thrown off its bogies and on to its side, and the body was torn from the frame. Considering that something like 200 people must have been crammed into the two coaches, it is remarkable that no more than thirty-one passengers were killed and forty-one others detained in hospital. Even so, it was by far the worst accident in the history of the Southern Railway. The total dead numbered thirty-two, for the motorman of the Tattenham Corner train was killed instantly. Once again we have to record a lucky escape by a guard, this time of the Haywards Heath train. His van in the rear coach was shattered, but he suffered only minor injuries

When Walder at the Junction heard the noise of the crash he phoned Hillier and asked if the Tattenham Corner train had run past his signals. 'No', came the reply. 'It was all my fault'.

I thought of those words as I stood on Purley Oaks station during the rush hour and watched the procession of trains passing through. Purley Oaks box has gone, and the automatic colour lights were ceaselessly changing. It seemed impossible that one signalman in a manually-operated box could ever have coped with that flood of traffic. That a man new to fog conditions should have forgotten one train became the most understandable thing in the world. The line is continuously track-circuited now, but ATC has not been installed.

Our sympathy goes out to Hillier, by consent of his colleagues and superiors a good man, and a very honest one. The lifelong memory of over thirty deaths is a heavy penalty to have to bear for a moment's forgetfulness. But at least he emerged without dishonour.

CHAPTER 23

GOSWICK

LONDON & NORTH EASTERN RAILWAY

This last great accident of the independent Companies took place on October 26, 1947, two days after the collision at South Croydon. In many ways it was another Bourne End. An express, due to be diverted for Sunday engineering work, disregarded the warning signals in clear daylight, took the turnout at a high speed and was derailed on a low embankment. Only in this case the driver and fireman lived to tell the tale, which from their point of view was not a creditable one. Therefore I shall not mention their names.

There was a third party on the footplate; an engine-crazy naval rating who had talked the driver into giving him a ride. Whether the presence of this illicit passenger had any bearing on the accident is uncertain, but it may have done.

Goswick, now closed, was a wayside station on the East Coast main line about seven miles south of Berwick. Between here and Beal, 2¾ miles to the south, are running loops in both directions for goods traffic, known for some reason as the independent lines. On this Sunday, because of bridge repairs, all traffic was being diverted on to these lines from the main line between seven in the morning and one o'clock. The work had been scheduled for the previous Sunday, but had been postponed.

In contrast to the fog which had shrouded London on the Friday, the weather in the north-east was bright and clear, with a south-easterly breeze blowing from off the North Sea.

The up signals at Goswick consisted of a distant placed far out (1,647 yards) from the home signal, doubtless on account of the falling gradient; the home signal 268 yards from the box, and splitting starters—main line, main-to-independent—close to the box itself. Signalman White, having had word that the engineer's gang was ready to start, set the road for the up independent line, bolted the points and put a collar on the lever. With the points set thus the distant signal was locked at caution and the up main starter at danger. The home signal and main-to-independent starter remained free of the interlocking. Between 7.30 a.m. and about mid-day five up goods trains passed, and White dealt with them in a way which proves him to have been a scrupulously careful signalman. The point involved was exactly the same as at Bourne End—how to warn a driver to reduce speed for a diversion. Under block telegraph regulations White would have been entitled to pull off his home signal and up-to-independent line starter as soon as he had accepted a train. But he preferred to operate the optional Rule 39 (a) and to keep his home signal at danger until the train was nearly at a standstill, and only then to pull off that signal and afterwards the starter, waiting generally in each case until the driver whistled. It was more trouble that way, for it meant keeping a close watch on the progress of each train, but White was the conscientious sort.

The scene shifts to Haymarket, one-time home shed of the unhappy Gourlay of Elliot Junction. The driver was going in by a back entrance, so as to avoid the timekeeper's and running foreman's office, for he had his unauthorised guest with him. This was the naval rating, who was wearing overalls borrowed from his fireman brother so as not to attract attention. He was not merely after a joy-ride; he wanted to learn. He was what one might call a locomotive addict, and having been a lifelong sufferer from the same complaint I feel a strong sympathy with him. He had been a porter at Waverley before being called up and had tried hard without success to transfer to the locomotive department. Now he was about to leave the Navy and had applied again, but had received no definite promise. Meanwhile he was desperately anxious to see a locomotive actually being fired en route. He had importuned the driver to let him travel on the footplate, and the driver, after refusing at first, had consented. It was a foolish thing to do, for a locomotive footplate is strictly forbidden ground for strangers. But our driver comes across as a weak and rather shifty character; exactly the sort of man who might yield to entreaties.

Having dispatched his guest to the engine, the driver proceeded to sign on and study the notices. It has been explained that the work at Goswick had been postponed from the previous Sunday; the change had appeared in the North-Eastern area printed notices but there had not been time to get it into the notices for the Scottish area. (We may well ask whether a phone call from Newcastle to Edinburgh would not have done the job). An amending notice had been dispatched from Newcastle on the Thursday but had been handled in leisurely fashion and did not reach the Haymarket shed until 11.25 on the Saturday. The office closed at noon, and it would seem that none of the young ladies could manage to type a brief notice in the thirty-five minutes available. So the time clerk wrote out a pencilled notice, which was put up on the 'late notices' board. There it was on the Sunday for our driver to see, but somehow he managed to miss it. The position of the board had been changed, but he had looked in the right place. He overlooked the pencilled sheet when a typewritten notice might have caught his eye. It was suggested at the inquiry that his preoccupation with his passenger prevented him from looking as closely as he should have done. So he set off from the shed unaware that he was to be diverted at Goswick.

The fireman also was unaware. He had arrived late and had had no time to look at the board.

So was the guard. In the guards' room at Waverley station all the late notices, including a number of old ones, were hung clipped together on a badly-illuminated board. The guard looked through the clip, but managed to miss this particular notice. So no one on the train knew of the diversion. That would not have mattered, of course, if the driver had observed the signals.

The day Scotsman left Waverley at 11.15 in the charge of A3 Pacific No. 66, 'Merry Hampton'. (For the benefit of the diesel generation I should explain that the L.N.E.R. named its A3 Pacifics after Derby winners. Racehorse owners are not given to calling their steeds King George III, King George IV and so on; they prefer more colourful names, some of which the L.N.E.R. had appropriated for this class. So we have 'Grand Parade' at Castlecary and 'Merry Hampton' here.) The train consisted of fifteen coaches, with 420 passengers—almost exactly the same as at Bourne End.

Just ninety minutes later, at 12.45, Signalman White received Train Entering Section for the Scotsman from Scremerston, the next box to the north. Following the same method as with the goods trains, he held his home signal at danger. The train first came into sight as it passed through an overbridge 1,457 yards from the box, a quarter of a mile beyond the distant, by which time it ought to have shut off steam. It was emitting steam, but White took it to be coming from the safety valve after the regulator had been closed. White had an almost directly head-on view of the train, which made it difficult for him to gauge its speed accurately. With steam shut off, as he supposed, he imagined it was slowing down. He allowed it to approach to within 360 yards of the home signal, which he then pulled off. He kept the starting signal at danger.

As the express was coming up to the home signal White realised that it was still steaming and travelling fast. He threw the home signal back to danger just before the train reached it; he said afterwards that he had seen the arm horizontal against the white background of the exhaust. I have said that the home signal was only 268 yards from the box; only 357 yards from the independent line turnout. Disaster was certain. 'Good God, he will not pull up', White exclaimed to the flagman who was having his dinner in the box. He did what he could. He used the emergency detonater placer and stood gesticulating at his window. The express appeared to have shut off steam when it passed him, but he did not think the brakes had been applied.

That was White's account. The driver's was different. He missed the distant, he said, because of steam blowing down on to the cab window. This may well have been the case, as the Pacifics were driven from the right, and a south-easterly wind would blow the exhaust to that side close to the engine. He put on the blower to try to lift the exhaust, but it failed to do so. Having missed the signal, he claimed, he shut off steam, but a moment later got a long sight of the home signal showing clear, and he did not therefore apply the brakes. He flatly contradicted White's evidence about both starting signals being at danger; one of them, he said—he could not remember which—was showing clear and was thrown to danger in his face. He did not explain why, with the vision on his own side obscured, he did not move across to the other side of the cab to observe the distant, or ask his fireman to do so.

Not surprisingly, the Inspector accepted White's account. How much of the driver's story was genuine self-deception of the kind we have noticed several times before, and how much plain lies, the reader may decide for himself.

The fireman was not looking for the signals because he was attending to the fire. He had let it drop during the descent from Grantshouse summit, and was now making it up again in readiness for the switchback road to Newcastle. But he also ought to have read the notice at the shed. He said at first that he had studied the board, but later admitted that he had come on duty too late to do so.

So 'Merry Hampton' took the facing points unchecked at a speed of at least 60 m.p.h. Turnouts on to goods lines are not laid out to be taken at any but the lowest speeds; this one had a 2-inch wrong way cant owing to the curvature of the main line and could not be negotiated safely at anything more than 15-20 m.p.h. The result was much the same as at Bourne End, except that the embankment was little more than a low bank with a ditch below. The engine turned over into the ditch with its wheels spinning, and eight of the leading nine vehicles followed it. Once again, as at Bourne End, a solitary vehicle—the fourth, the leading coach of the triplet dining car set—went its own way along the track and skidded to a standstill seventy yards ahead. But compared with Bourne End there was one important difference. All the vehicles had buckeye couplings and Pullman vestibules (except for the intermediate couplings of the triplet set) and from the seventh coach rearwards all the couplings held, even on those vehicles which had lost their bogies. The leading coaches were strewn around, but more or less together; there was no telescoping and no pile of wreckage as at Bourne End. Perhaps we may give the couplinges credit for the lower loss of life than in that disaster, but it was serious enough. The killed numbered twenty-eight, including a train attendant.

Both the driver and fireman were severely hurt and spent several months in hospital. What awaited them on their return I do not know; for the driver a severe disciplining at the least, if not dismissal. Whatever his punishment, no doubt he deserved it. But we may spare a thought for the sailor, who was also badly hurt. Not only had his eagerly-sought trip ended in tragedy, but he had doubtless forfeited for ever the prospect of a career among his beloved engines.

CHAPTER 24

WINSFORD
LONDON MIDLAND REGION, B.R.

This might be called the story of the soldier who wanted his wife, or of the signalman who wanted his supper. Though neither circumstance actually caused the accident—well, the supper episode may have done—without both the accident would not have occurred. It happened about half an hour after midnight on 17th April, 1948; it was the newly-formed British Railways' first big accident.

Travelling in the 5.40 p.m. express from Glasgow was an artilleryman aged 19, married and irresponsible. He was an ex-railwayman who before joining up had worked in Winsford Junction box, which he was just passing. He was on leave, in love and less than a mile from home—his in-laws' home, to be exact. Why be carried on to Crewe, he reasoned, eight miles further on, and have to wait until seven o'clock next morning for a train back, when there was a perfectly good communication cord? So he went into the toilet and pulled it, and when the train had come to a standstill he slipped away across the moonlit fields. As a former railwayman he knew all about how a standing train is protected, and so of course should this train have been. As it was, he bought the extra night with his wife at a cost of twenty-four lives. It is to his credit that after the accident he came forward and owned up.

From Winsford Junction to Winsford station is a block section of about 1½ miles. The express came to a stop about 1,200 yards before Winsford station and—unfortunately—650 yards short of the track circuit which would have given the signalman a continuing reminder of the train's presence. The fireman, Price, got down from the footplate of Princess Pacific No. 6207 and began to walk back along the train, examining the coach ends as he went for the turned disc marking the coach in which the cord had been pulled. The guard meanwhile had been walking up the other way, examining the vacuum pipe and generally trying to find out what was amiss. I shall call the guard Sandy; he was sixty-three and he appears as a well-meaning and rather clumsy figure, with an unbelievably broad Scottish accent. A train making an emergency stop has to be protected without delay, and the rules lay down that it is the guard's duty, apart from one circumstance. This is when the communication cord has been pulled. Then the guard must seek out the passenger who pulled it and find out what he wants, while the fireman goes back to protect the train. This consists of laying detonators at stated intervals and displaying a hand signal—a night, a red lamp. However Sandy, in his wisdom, decided that he was the more experienced man to go back. He told Price to continue looking for the coach, while he returned to his van for detonators and set off to the rear. It might have been better if he and Price had stuck to their prescribed tasks, for he managed to trip over a sleeper and his lamp went out. All this had taken a good deal longer than he realized, and having to re-light his lamp made it longer still. In fact the express had been standing for seventeen minutes, and there was another train following behind. Sandy had only had time to go about 400 yards and lay a couple of detonators before the following train was upon him.

This was the up Glasgow Postal, running late. It should have passed the express at Lancaster, but the latter had been allowed to go forward. Driver Howie, in charge of Pacific No. 6251 'City of Nottingham', was making up time along the level track, probably doing nearer 70 than 60 m.p.h. He had passed Winsford Junction under clear signals when he saw a red light being waved by the track and heard the crack of a detonator. He immediately shut off steam and applied the brakes—we observe some quick action here—but could only bring down his speed to about 45 m.p.h. before he crashed into the rear of the stationary express.

Let us look at what had been happening in the signal boxes. At Winsford Junction was Signalman Chamberlain, a man of sixty-six and old to be still at work. But he was fully alert. He had sent Train Entering Section to Winsford Station box for the express as it had passed his box at 12.9 a.m., and on this short block section he expected the Train Out Of Section signal a minute or two later. But no signal came. After five minutes, at 12.14 a.m. he phoned the man at Winsford Station, who plays the principal part in this story and whom I shall call Harris. Harris replied that he had missed the tail lamp, as a goods train passing in the other direction had blocked his view. This seemed odd to Chamberlain, as the goods in question had already reached Winsford Junction and must have passed Winsford station some minutes before the express could have got there. However he supposed that Harris, having missed the tail lamp, was 'holding the block' as required by the rules and was waiting to get clearance from Minshull Vernon, the next box ahead, before clearing back to Winsford Junction. When Harris sent Train Out Of Section at 12.17 a.m. Chamberlain was entirely satisfied. At 12.22 a.m. he offered the Postal to Harris, who accepted it at once. It passed the box at 12.26 a.m. and a minute or so later Chamberlain heard a dull thud. He thought no more of it until he saw a red light approaching along the line, and Sandy entered in a state of high emotion with a tale of which Chamberlain could hardly understand a word.

There must have been something rather comical in the confrontation of the two elderly men; Sandy in much agitation mouthing his incoherent brogue, Chamberlain utterly uncomprehending. It appeared that something dreadful had happened, but it was only when Guard Horne of the Postal reached the box ten minutes later that Chamberlain realized there had been a collision. Horne distinguished himself on this night. He had been thrown to the floor and received chest injuries, but he had made his way to the box and afterwards returned to the accident, where he set a passenger's broken arm in splints before receiving attention himself.

Let us pause in our story to notice a pathetic figure, one of the victims of modernization. Chamberlain's booking 'lad'— a job normally entrusted to a young boy—was another signalman of sixty, who had been put on to this work after his own box had been closed. It was better by far of course than being out of work, but it was a sad end to a lifetime in the railway service, and it gives us an insight into the human aspect of redundancy. He died shortly after giving evidence at the inquiry.

We move now to Winsford Station box and meet Harris, another elderly man of sixty-two. He was well regarded by his superiors, but it would be fair to say that he was not the man he had been. A signalman suffers from the occupational hazards of hernia and indidigestion—the first due to stiff levers and the second to having to bolt his meals in the intervals between passing trains. As a young man I once lodged with a signalman's family and saw how devastating the effect can be. Harris had had a hernia operation three years earlier, and we may suspect that he was liable to indigestion. That seems the most likely reason for his preoccupation with his midnight hot supper, for his box remarkably contained a cooking stove. At this moment too he was under the weather with a cold, and he had been anxious about his wife's health. All this adds up to a man more than usually liable to commit an error. He seems to have fallen into the weary man's habit of doing his job by rote—in the Inspector's words, attending to block signals as a matter of routine—rather than bothering to keep track of trains as they passed his box.

Harris's own account of the night's events need not concern us. His explanations were confused and showed a lack of honesty with himself, as the Inspector charitably put it. We can piece together fairly well what actually happened. At the time when Train Entering Section was given from Winsford Junction Harris was about to take his meal from the oven, while the kettle was also boiling. That, let us recall, was at 12.9 a.m. and he was anxious to get the express disposed of before starting his meal. Possibly he did not want the meal overcooked; at all event his mind was more on his supper than on the train. So two minutes later, at 12.11 a.m. by which time the express should have passed, he assumed that it had actually done so. We know this because he entered it as such in his register at that time and sent Train Entering Section at the same time to Minshull Vernon. He had somehow managed to persuade himself that the express's tail lamp really had been obscured by the goods train, but that it had definitely passed his box. This seems to have been genuine self-delusion, for he repeated the story to the fireman Price when the latter came into the box. It should be said in Harris's favour that he admitted that he was responsible for the accident.

Meanwhile at Minshull Vernon Signalman Morris was wondering what had happened to the express. From Winsford was only a four minutes' run, so it should have passed his box at 12.15 a.m. He thought it might have been checked in Winsford station, so at 12.16 a.m. he phoned Harris to ask if it was 'doing all right'. Harris replied: 'Yes'. Morris left his box and looked along the line, and as he still could see no train he took the precaution of stopping the down Postal, which was approaching his box at that moment, and cautioning the driver. This procedure is required by the regulations when a train has been an unusually long time in a section, and by carrying it out Morris prevented a double collision of the Quintinshill pattern.

Thus Harris had been reminded twice, by Chamberlain's call

at 12.14 a.m. and by Morris's two minutes later. Possibly shaken in his belief by these calls, he went down on to the line, but seeing nothing—the standing express was hidden from his view by an overbridge—his conviction re-asserted itself, and he cleared back at 12.17 a.m. as has been described. Five minutes later he accepted the Postal.

The situation was now the same as it had been at Welwyn. A train still in the section had been wrongly cleared back and a following train accepted, and as at Welwyn there was no safeguard against this contingency. If the train had reached the home signal track circuit the indicator in Harris's box would have shown 'occupied' and reminded Harris of its presence. But if the Welwyn Control, widely adopted by the L.N.E.R. after the accident, had been in operation here, it would have been impossible for Harris to accept the Postal train. For the Welwyn Control ensures that once a train has been accepted from the rear the 'berth'—home signal—track circuit must be occupied *and cleared* before another train can be accepted. At Winsford, as it happened, the Inspector's recommendation on this point became academic, since the signalling was totally reorganized when the line was electrified. But we may wonder how many Winsfords had been prevented on the L.N.E.R. by the Welwyn Control. We never hear about the accidents that do not happen.

We return to the scene of the collision. When Price and his driver had at last located and restored the turned disc—it was on the third coach—the train's brakes came off, as the driver had kept on his small ejector for this purpose. The shock of the impact was thus to that extent lessened, but the 45 m.p.h. crunch turned the rear coach into a mass of wreckage, which telescoped the rear part of the coach in front. All the dead were in these two coaches; beyond that there was little damage. But the shock wave broke the couplings behind the sixth coach, an action which applied the brake again by breaking the pipe. On the Postal train the second, third and fourth vehicles were badly telescoped, but the leading vehicle, a G.W.R. milk van (how did it come to be on a Postal train?) was, freakishly, but little damaged.

The nearest houses are some distance away, but we read that then and there, in the middle of the night, over ninety homes in the neighbourhood were thrown open to the victims and the stranded. We have an echo of continuing post-war austerity in the Railway Executive's announcement that 'the people who so unselfishly divided their rations with strangers would be compensated'—in rations, let us hope.

We shall hear of Winsford again, for it is the most recent addition to the list of two-disaster spots. How a fully-modernized, continuously colour-lighted and track-circuited, automatic-train-controlled stretch of line could still manage to become the scene of a great disaster, remarkably similar to the one described here, will be recounted in our final chapter.

CHAPTER 25

HARROW

LONDON MIDLAND REGION, B.R.

We return for our next accident to Greater London, for the second of the sequence of great London disasters of which I have spoken. Harrow and Wealdstone is the official title, for it occurred actually in the station of that name. I shall call it Harrow for short. It happened on October 8, 1952 at 8.18½ a.m.; we know the time so exactly because the shock of the collision stopped all the station clocks.

Even among great disasters Harrow holds a special place. It shares two distinctions, if I may use the term, with Quintinshill. Like that earlier tragedy, it was a double collision. It is also the only other British accident in which the number of dead ran into three figures. Even so it fails to challenge that ultimate horror of long ago, for its 112 lives lost numbered less than half the death-roll at Quintinshill.

Quintinshill has passed into history, a fading memory with a few elderly people. The memory of Harrow is still vivid in the minds of many in the prime of life. Yet in a sense it too already belongs to history. It was the last great all-steam accident. Where it took place no steam engine is ever likely to run again, save perhaps occasionally with an enthusiasts' special. So it was appropriate that one of the locomotives destroyed in the collision should have been one that had been used as an experiment to perpetuate the life of steam. We shall come to that in a moment.

Harrow has some remarkable parallels with Bourne End, less than fifteen miles away. The same train was involved—the night express from Perth. Both accidents took place on a calm autumn morning, though at Harrow there was some mist about. In both cases the driver disregarded the warning of both the colour light distant and the home semaphore signals. Both engine crews perished, leaving us to wonder exactly what happened. But whereas Bourne

End remains a baffling mystery, there is at least a reasonable explanation in the case of Harrow.

The Perth express had changed since Bourne End. Its fifteen vehicles had shrunk to eleven and its passenger complement—symptom of the decline in railway travel—from nearly 400 to a mere eighty-five. It had been speeded up, and in place of a Royal Scot it was hauled by Pacific No. 46262, 'City of Glasgow', sister engine to 'City of Nottingham' involved at Winsford. Its driver Jones, of Crewe North shed, was only forty-three. He was known at Crewe as a 'methodical young man', who was in the habit of attending improvement classes. His fireman, Turnock, aged twenty-three, was a keen, steady type, 'out to build himself up to be a good driver', as one of his instructors put it.

Approaching Harrow from the other direction, fairly well filled with about 200 passengers, was the 8 a.m. express from Euston to Liverpool and Manchester, consisting of fifteen vehicles double-headed by Jubilee 4-6-0 No. 45637, working back to its home shed at Edge Hill, with Pacific No. 46202 'Princess Anne' as train engine. The latter, as I have hinted, was an engine with a history. It had spent most of its career as a turbine-driven locomotive. The idea of applying the steam turbine, so successful at sea, to railway operation had haunted locomotive engineers, and from about 1908 onwards various experimental turbine locomotives had been built in Britain and elsewhere. On trial they performed very well, but not so much better than a conventional engine as to justify the extra trouble and expense. No. 6202—as she was in L.M.S. days—was chosen for conversion into a non-condensing turbine engine, to try to eliminate the clumsy condenser. She was no failure, but when I encountered her at Euston one day I found that she always had to carry a third man, a fitter, to keep things in order. She had been converted back to normal only a few months earlier, and on this morning was making her last journey, for she was too badly damaged to be worth repairing.

The Perth express had been having a bad run. From Wigan southwards it had been travelling through continuous fog; the driver of a preceding Glasgow train said that visibility was hardly more than fifty yards the whole way. Already thirty-two minutes late leaving Crewe, the express was now running eighty minutes behind time. But as it approached London the fog began to grow less dense. By the time Harrow was reached visibility had risen to between 100 and

300 yards—not enough to interfere seriously with the observation of signals.

Jones was coasting down the long descent from Bushey with regulator closed at 55-60 m.p.h. He had just shown himself fully alert by observing a signal stop at the north entrance to Watford tunnel and 15 m.p.h. p.w. restriction in the tunnel itself. At Bushey, where the fog was dense enough to warrant a fogman at the semaphore distant, Jones had waved to him. He was the last man to see Jones alive.

We now join Signalman Armitage in Harrow No. 1 box, on the country side of Harrow station and controlling the crossover there. Armitage was aged thirty-four, and his first box on re-joining the railway after leaving the Army had been, strangely enough, Bourne End. He was now a relief signalman covering a number of boxes— a responsible position, for the relief man must be familiar with the working of them all. He was described as sensitive, and was badly shocked by the spectacle of the collision, but he showed that he knew how to act like a good signalman. When he had come on duty at 6 o'clock his 'fog object'—the back light of his home signal 303 yards distant—had been visible, but by 6.35 it had been obscured, and since no fogman was available he had resorted to fog working—a matter, as at Eccles and South Croydon, of holding trains further back from an approach to converging lines. At 8.10 however the sun was beginning to break through; he could see his 'fog object' again and resumed normal working.

Approaching on the up slow line was the 7.31 local from Tring, hauled by Class 4 2-6-4T No. 42389 running bunker first. Owing to the fog it was about five minutes behind time. It was scheduled to cross over the fast line at Harrow, in order to leave the up slow line clear for the morning procession of empty stock movements into Euston from Stonebridge Park sidings. All railway managements give high priority to the punctuality of their suburban services, so the orders were to give these trains precedence over any night express that might be running late, even if it meant delaying the latter by a further two or three minutes. The local was therefore to cross over in front of the express.

Armitage accepted the local from Hatch End on the slow line at 8.7 a.m. and at 8.11 a.m. he accepted the Perth express on the fast line up to his outer home signal, as he was entitled to do under normal working. (If it had been one minute earlier, when fog working was still in force, he would not have been able to accept it at all.) He received Train Entering Section for the local at 8.14 a.m., and after a goods train had passed his box on the down slow line he reversed the points for the crossover. Like White at Goswick, Armitage was an ultra-careful signalman who took greater precautions than the rules demanded. Until the Bourne End accident, under L.M.S. regulations, the splitting distant and home signals were regarded as sufficient warning of a diversion; after that accident the rule was altered in the case of out-of-course diversions, when the signalman had to keep the home signal at danger until the train was nearly at a standstill. But Armitage applied the rule to booked diversions also, as in this case. That had no bearing on the accident, but it shows him as a highly conscientious signalman.

The local duly crossed over to the fast line and came to a stop in Harrow station at 8.17 a.m.

The Liverpool train had been late leaving Euston, but with such power available it was making up time, and was mounting the 1 in 339 gradient at much the same speed as the Perth train was approaching downhill, namely 55-60 m.p.h. Armitage received Train Entering Section for both trains at 8.17 a.m. About a minute later he was astonished to hear the Perth express approaching at speed; then it came out of the mist by the outer home signal, making no attempt to stop. With only seconds available, Armitage gave a copybook demonstration of how a signalman should act in an emergency. He pulled his lever to place a detonator on the line in the path of the Perth train and threw his signals to danger in front of the Liverpool train. But at that moment the annunciator buzzer sounded in the box, showing that the Liverpool train had reached the track circuit in rear of the home signal, just at the south end of the station platform. His efforts had been in vain.

Armitage was now the compulsory witness of a scene only rivalled by that observed by the guilty pair at Quintinshill. No wonder after the accident the stationmaster found him deathly white. The two collisions were practically simultaneous. The Perth train had hardly crashed into the rear of the standing local, shattering the last three coaches, when the Liverpool train ploughed into the wreckage.

The Tring train was more than usually full, for another train had been cancelled that morning on account of track and signalling work at Euston. It arrived at Harrow with about two-thirds of the seats taken, and waiting for it were 332 passengers—we know the number exactly because a census was being taken. It now contained some 800 passengers or about eleven to a compartment—a big crowd for the Euston line, though quite normal in the case, say, of the Southern Electric. The train had been standing for about 1½ minutes, and the carriage doors were being closed, when the passengers in the fore part felt three heavy shocks as the Perth train destroyed the three rear coaches in succession. The local was standing with its brakes off, but was only driven forward about an engine's length. Its guard, Merritt, was still on the platform when he caught sight of the express coming. He ran across to the other side, jumped down on to the track and took refuge under the platform coping until the noise of the collision had died away. He was on duty the next day with a bottle of tonic to steady his nerves.

'City of Glasgow' was deflected to the right and came to rest on its side on the down main line, right in the path of the Liverpool train. The Jubilee at the head of the latter struck it full-on. The crunch between a 700-ton fast-moving mass and a 100-ton obstacle produced destruction on a spectacular scale. The Jubilee was thrown to the left clean across the platform, where it swept to their death passengers waiting for the next electric train. It landed on its side across the electric lines, the ruin of an engine. It was followed by 'Princess Anne', likewise shattered, though the crew survived. Not even modern stock could withstand the force of such a collision. The L.M.S. had not followed the L.N.E.R.'s example of standardizing buckeye couplings—though one or two new B.R. coaches in the Liverpool express were so fitted—but it is doubtful if any form of construction could have survived the shock. Sixteen vehicles were destroyed or practically so—five in the Perth train, three in the local and eight in the Liverpool train. Thirteen of these were piled into a heap of wreckage forty-five yards long by eighteen yards wide by thirty feet high, burying 'City of Glasgow' and its dead crew. One corner of the pile struck the footbridge spanning the platforms and brought down a girder to add to the wreck. The driver of the leading engine was killed, but the fireman had a remarkable escape. Somehow he was thrown clear, and when he came to he found himself on the upturned wheel splasher of the train engine.

Four of the dead were railwaymen—the two drivers and fireman as described, and an attendant on the Liverpool train. Of the 108 passengers killed it was estimated that sixty-four were in the local, twenty-three in the Perth express and seven in the Liverpool train. The remaining fourteen were probably waiting on the up electric line platform. Considering that three out of the nine coaches of the local were destroyed, the death roll—no more than 8 per cent of the passengers in it—was remarkably small. The explanation is doubtless that, after the manner of commuters in the morning, the passengers had crowded to the front. Thirty-six of the dead in this train were members of the railway staff travelling to work at the L.M.R. headquarters at Euston.

The two leading vehicles of the Perth train consisted of vans, which helped to keep down casualties, but the number of dead, more than one-quarter of all the passengers in the train, was remarkably high and hard to explain. By contrast it was astonishing that only eight were killed in the tangled wreckage of the first eight coaches of the Liverpool train.

If accidents must happen, it is a great advantage that they should do so in a built-up area. Housewives flooded to the scene with torn-up sheets, which they proceeded to roll into bandages, and with hot drinks for the injured and shocked. But the accident will be best remembered for the help once again given by the Americans. It was on an even more massive scale that at Bourne End. From the U.S. Air Force headquarters at Ruislip, from the depots and airfields at Bushey Park, West Drayton and Bovingdon, came 500 doctors and nurses with all their superb equipment—ambulances, mobile first-aid posts, portable dispensaries, on-the-spot transfusion units. As the *Daily Mirror* wrote: 'The injured didn't have to wait to go to hospital for treatment—the hospital came to them'. I for one long remember the picture of the coloured nurse from Florida, Abbie Sweetwine, cradling a badly hurt passenger while the American doctor attends to him, also the Boston sergeant's comment on the behaviour of the injured: 'The British don't cry'.

To the Inspecting Officer, Lt. Col. Wilson, fell the task of trying to probe the cause of the disaster. He examined a number of possibilities. Could the driver have been taken ill? Had he mistaken the signals on the electric line, which return to normal at green, for his own? Had there been a blow-back? Had the exhaust from the passing goods train obscured the distant signal? Could the driver have been blinded by the sun, which just then was beginning to rise above the mist? Had Signalman Armitage decided first to give the express precedence and then changed his mind? All these possibilities had to be discarded. But the Inspector came up with a suggested explanation, feasible if purely conjectural. Remember that Swaby at Bourne End had managed to disregard two sets of warning signals for at least twenty seconds each. In the present case Driver Jones, in the prevailing conditions of visibility, had possibly only four seconds in which to observe the colour light distant, though for that time it would shine with increasing brilliance. If Jones had missed it without realising he had done so, he might have continued to look out for it at its height of fourteen feet above the ground, and thus have missed the outer and inner home semaphores, set at a height of thirty feet and more. In that case only when the surroundings of Harrow station came into view would he have realized where he was—it was established that the brakes were applied a few seconds before the crash. The fireman would have had no cause to be looking out for the signals, as they were on the left-hand—the driver's—side.

Harrow was another accident which could have been prevented by Automatic Train Control, and the Inspector once again dealt with the subject at length. His remarks go some way to explain, if not altogether to excuse, British Railways' tardiness in coming to a decision. The independent Companies may fairly be criticized for not following the Great Western's lead, but by the time they came to be nationalized the picture had changed. Not unnaturally, it was desired to use a standardized system, and the G.W.R. system was found to be unsuitable for electrified lines. I need not go into details; suffice to say that a prototype had been agreed only two months before the Harrow accident, though final Ministry approval had to wait until 1956. But the Harrow report put the subject into perspective. The Inspector gave an analysis of 640 accidents involving fatalities between 1912 and 1952; this showed that only 10 per cent of the accidents would have been prevented by Warning Control, though they accounted for 28 per cent of the deaths. Both figures are lower than might have been supposed from a reading of this book, where the subject inevitably has loomed large. Quintinshill of course was a notable case which would not have been prevented; Warning Control, let us remember, offers no protection against a signalman's mistakes. One interesting revelation in the report takes us back to Castlecary. After that accident, we learn, the L.N.E.R. began to instal A.T.C. between Glasgow and Edinburgh, but the work was brought to a stop by the war.

But protection against error is not the only benefit to be derived from an Automatic Warning System (A.W.S.), as it is now officially called. More important in day-to-day operation is its ability to speed up operation in fog. How well it can do this I saw for myself only a short while ago, when in dense fog between Reading and Maidenhead we maintained a steady 80 m.p.h. And yet the Region which has most to gain from aids to fog operation—the Southern—is still without A.W.S.

The layout at Harrow has been altered since the accident, and the crossover has been transferred to the London end of the station. Had this been so at the time the accident would not have occurred, for the Tring train would have been standing at the slow line platform and the express would have been given a run-through. The signal box has disappeared, along with all the other station signal boxes on the route; the entire length is now controlled from the brand-new box at Willesden. Apart from these, and the catenary, the scene is unchanged. The footbridge, strangely, bears no trace of the bashing it took. Harrow and Wealdstone, scene of a great calamity, is a very ordinary suburban station.

CHAPTER 26

LEWISHAM

SOUTHERN REGION, B.R.

The brick wilderness of the south-eastern suburbs provides the setting for our last great London accident—it is to be hoped the last-ever. Lewisham St. Johns is its official name, for it happened just beyond the far end of St. Johns station in Lewisham Borough. I shall use its usual short title of Lewisham. It was the closest-in of our three London accidents; the 5¾ mile post from Charing Cross stands just by the site. It happened during the evening rush hour, at 6.20 on 4th December 1957, when a bank of dense fog rolled down the hill from Blackheath on to the railway between New Cross and St. Johns.

In the five years since Harrow London had not been accident-free. On 8th April 1953 London Transport suffered its one and only deep-level tube collision. This was on the Central Line between Stratford and Leyton; in the confined space of a tube tunnel it was a very nasty affair, and twelve people were killed. Two and a half years later, on 2nd December 1955, a Southern Region Windsor-bound electric ran into the rear of a stationary goods train at night, near Barnes. The leading coach caught fire, and thirteen lives were lost.

Both these were minor accidents compared with Lewisham, in which ninety lives were lost. It thus ranks behind Quintinshill and Harrow as the third-worst British railway accident. Like a number of the other accidents described in this book, it was a rear-end collision; a steam train ran into the back of a stationary electric train. But it had one unusual feature. It took place almost directly beneath an overbridge, which collapsed on to the wreckage. Much the same thing had happened at Harrow, but that was only a footbridge and so far as is known it caused no additional casualties. The bridge at St. Johns was a two-span girder structure carrying the Nunhead—Lewisham connection over the main lines, and its fall made a bad

accident worse. If I may reminisce for a moment, I remember that
bridge. It had collapsed once before, when it was being built in 1929.
I was living in Eltham at the time, and I shall not forget the wild
chaos at Charing Cross as passengers surged from platform to platform seeking a train which would take them home. I finally landed
up at Mottingham and walked it.

As at South Croydon ten years before, responsibility for the accident was placed on a single individual, in this case the driver of the
steam train. But just as with Hillier at South Croydon, it seems to
me that he bears no moral blame. The worst that can be said of
him is that he failed to react with sufficient speed to a surprise situation, as we have seen a number of drivers had done before him. Yet
in addition to the agony of having been the instrument of disaster,
he had to undergo the further ordeal of two trials, though not
fortunately of a sentence. If any driver deserves our sympathy he
does, and I see no reason why I should not mention his name.

Our story opens at Cannon Street shortly before six o'clock.
Driver Trew and Fireman Hoare, of Ramsgate, had been shivering
for over an hour on the fog-bound and freezing platform, waiting
for their train complete with engine to be hauled in, after the manner of steam working at Cannon Street. This was the 4.56 p.m. to
Ramsgate via Folkstone—in effect the same train as the 5 p.m.
which had been derailed at Sevenoaks thirty years before, as
described in Chapter 13. Trew and Hoare had arrived at Charing
Cross from their home shed at 4.10 p.m. and after a quick meal
in the staff canteen had made haste to go across to Cannon Street,
just in case the 4.56 p.m. should be ready to leave on time. They
would have done better to stay in the canteen. Their engine, Battle
of Britain Class light Pacific No. 34066, 'Spitfire', was shedded at
Stewart's Lane, Battersea, the old L.C. & D. shed—a mere three
or four miles from Cannon Street as the crow flies, but requiring a
roundabout fifteen-mile or so journey. It had left Stewart's Lane at
3.15 p.m. in the charge of a shed crew, travelling via Nunhead and
Blackheath to Charlton, over the very bridge which it was to bring
down less than three hours later, then back tender first through
Greenwich to be attached to its train at Rotherhithe Road carriage
sidings, and so with a fresh crew, and an engine at both ends, to
Cannon Street. The whole journey, which should have taken about
1¼ hours, had taken more than double that time because of the

fog, and it was five minutes to six before Trew and Hoare were at last able to board their engine.

I should not have liked to be in Trew's place. The Battle of Britain Pacifics, like the larger Merchant Navy class, were fitted with side sheets to the boiler, for no better reason than that their designer considered it gave them a 'modern' look. Some of both classes had been rebuilt without the side sheets, but 'Spitfire' was not one of them. These sheets obstructed the look-out, which was further restricted by a narrow 8' 6" cab to enable the engines to work through the Bo-Beep tunnel on the Hastings line. To have charge of such an engine on a foggy night must in itself have been no small strain.

Owing to the long delay in reaching Cannon Street the water in the tank was low, and Trew gave notice that he intended to make a stop for water at Sevenoaks.

The 4.56 finally got away at 6.8 p.m., 72 minutes late, over-filled with 700 passengers who had accumulated during the long wait. For the first 3½ miles to New Cross all went well. The line is continuously on viaduct and the fog was less dense than at ground level. Each successive colour light showed green, and Trew was able to keep going at 30–35 m.p.h. The light at the far end of New Cross platform, A42, was likewise at green. Then suddenly, without warning, as is the way with fog at night, the train plunged into the opaque blackness of the cutting beyond.

We must now see what had been happening just over a mile further on at Parks Bridge Junction, where the mid-Kent line for Hayes and Addiscombe diverges to the right from the main line. Halted at the junction lights was the 5.25 p.m. Charing Cross to Hastings diesel, and halted at the previous light, 476 yards in rear, was the 5.18 p.m. electric train from Charing Cross to Hayes, its ten coaches crammed to bursting with 1,500 passengers. As the times show, these trains were running in their wrong order owing to the fog. The Hastings train need not have been stopped, but Signalman Beckett at Parks Bridge was under the impression that it was the Hayes train, and had therefore halted it to allow a train on the up main line to pass. The reasons for the misunderstanding are worth explaining, because they are a perfect example of how small circumstances can lead to great disasters. The Hastings service had only lately been dieselized, and there was no separate space on the 'describer' (the box-to-box route indicator) to distinguish it from a main line electric. Such a train—to Orpington—had just passed, and Beckett had missed the next—identical—'description' from St. Johns for the Hastings train. Thus it was he came to believe that it was the Hayes train standing at his signals, and a phone call to the box from the Hastings driver did not remove his misapprehension, perhaps because the Hayes driver also phoned at just about the same time. Probably the mistake would not have occurred if Beckett had had a booking boy as he should have done. But boy labour, as employers know, is hard to come by in London. Beckett was of course in no sense responsible for the accident, but if he had got his trains right both the Hastings and Hayes trains would have been on their way, and there would have been no collision.

One hundred and thirty-eight yards in rear of the tail of the Hayes train was colour light L18, of course showing red. Behind it, at roughly quarter-mile intervals, were lights L17 and L16, correctly showing one and two yellows respectively. Behind L16 again was the New Cross light A42, which Trew had just passed at green. All these lights were on the right-hand side, the fireman's side in this class of engine, but in clear weather L16 and L17 could first be seen by the driver because of the left-hand curve. But the long boiler with its side sheets cut off his view eighty yards away or even further, and here was visibility suddenly reduced to a mere twenty yards or so. A quick-thinking man might have called out to his fireman to look out for these two signals, as the driver of the preceding steam train had done. But Trew, though steady and conscientious, was no quick thinker, in which respect he differed not at all from a number of other drivers we have encountered, who were not held blameworthy. His statements afterwards were confused—small wonder—but I believe we can follow his thoughts. He had had the green at New Cross, and he had never before been checked at any of the succeeding lights, which he took for granted would be showing clear. If I read his character aright, this was not a conscious assumption, or in any sense a deliberate disregard of the lights. The possibility that they might be at caution simply did not cross his mind—or did not do so in time. Because of that he brought about the accident. One may say that it should have crossed his mind, since every driver knows that it is his first duty to observe the signals, but how many of us could be certain that, caught unawares, we should not suffer the same sort of mental blockage? His conduct was in a very different category from that of the bemused Aldington—as we have supposed him to be—at Charfield, or the sheer stupidity of the driver in our next chapter.

The stop at Sevenoaks, too, was on Trew's mind. He was anxious to make as good a run as he could so that too much time might not be lost—in normal circumstances a wholly praiseworthy aim.

So lights L16 and L17 were missed. At L18 Hoare was looking out, 'Red', he called across to Trew. With the tail of the Hayes train 138 yards ahead, instant action might still have prevented the collision or reduced its violence. The line rises at this point at 1 in 218, and calculations showed that at 30 m.p.h. the train could have been stopped in 130 yards. Trew shut off steam and applied the brake, but not quickly enough to make much difference. His train was still travelling at about 30 m.p.h. when it struck the Hayes train. The latter was standing with the brakes on to hold it on the gradient; a near-immovable 400-ton obstacle.

'Spitfire' embedded itself in the rear coach of the Hayes train, killing the guard, but it was the eighth coach that suffered most. It was overridden by the ninth coach and the bodywork destroyed. The damage to the Ramsgate train was still worse. The rear of the electric train was standing just ahead of the overbridge, and the engine's tender and the leading coach were flung against one of the stanchions, bringing down two of the heavy girders on to the still-moving train. The second coach and half the third were crushed beneath their weight. Strange to say, No. 34066 kept the rails, though its front end was badly damaged.

A driver and fireman who were travelling in the Hayes train went back to the engine and threw out the fire. They found Trew still on the footplate, unhurt but badly shocked. They helped him down the bank to a nearby house, from which he was taken to hospital; he returned home the next day. The fireman was badly injured.

Ninety people, as has been said, lost their lives. Of the eighty-nine passengers killed, thirty-seven were known to be in the Hayes train and forty-nine in the Ramsgate train—the casualties in the latter certainly swollen by the collapse of the bridge girders. Once again, as at Harrow, one is moved to remark on the comparative fewness of the number killed, at all events in the Hayes train. Considering that one of its coaches, which must have held some 150 people, was totally destroyed, and two others badly damaged, a total of thirty-seven dead seems unbelievably small. Even taking into account the number of injured detained in hospital—109 in the two trains together—it means that one could have been sitting (or standing) in a coach that was utterly pulverized and yet had at least a fifty-fifty chance of escaping death or serious injury.

I have yet to mention that the accident was very nearly a double collision of a most peculiar sort. That was prevented in the nick of time by a driver's alertness and quick thinking. The Nunhead—Lewisham route which crossed the bridge was originally intended for goods traffic between the Northern lines and Hither Green sidings, but it was later electrified to carry a rush-hour service between Holborn Viaduct and Dartford. Two minutes after the accident Motorman Corke was approaching the bridge with the 5.22 from Holborn Viaduct, when peering ahead through the mist he noticed that the girders were tilting. Quick as thought he cut off power and braked, and managed to bring his train to a standstill on the shelving track, with its leading coach actually above the mangled vehicles of the Ramsgate train. Any less prompt action would have caused the train to be precipitated on to the wreckage below.

As I have hinted, there was a harrowing sequel for Trew. The Inspecting Officer, while bound to hold him responsible, showed an understanding of the man and the circumstances. But the Coroner's jury took a different view, and Trew found himself on a charge of manslaughter. At the first trial on April 21st the jury disagreed—it would be fascinating to know how the voting went—but at the re-trial on May 8th the Crown offered no evidence. After five months Trew's ordeal was over.

Of the Lewisham accident we can say for certain that it would not have happened with diesel or electric traction. With no boiler to obstruct his view, the driver would have had a clear sight of each light as he came up to it. On another point, Trew would not have been anxious about the water stop, which may have helped to distract his thoughts. Among the many benefits derived from modern motive power extra safety is by no means the least. When the South-Eastern section is equipped in due course with the Automatic Warning System it will be as near a hundred per cent accident-proof as is humanly possible. But while human frailty persists total immunity is not within our power to achieve, as our next and last accident all too painfully illustrates.

CHAPTER 27

WINSFORD No. 2
LONDON MIDLAND REGION, B.R.

It is the evening of Boxing Day, 1962. Once again we are at Winsford, scene of the collision of 1948, only this time on the other side of the station, about a couple of miles nearer Crewe. Once again it is dark. Once again an up express is standing halted while another train follows, with the same tragic result. Only this time it is a driver who was at fault—a fault so crass a to be scarcely believable.

Here at last British Railways have fully emerged into the new age. For the first time where main line trains are involved no steam locomotive is concerned. The line is electrified, though trains from the Carlisle direction are diesel-hauled. It is a very different Winsford, too, from the one we encountered fourteen years before. The station is still there, together with the box in which the senescent Harris had been so preoccupied with his midnight supper, but the signals have gone, replaced by continuous colour lights operated at the boxes by the signalman and automatically in between. The line is continuously track-circuited, with circuit indications and telephone lines connecting in every case with the box ahead—in this case Coppenhall Junction in the up direction and Winsford in the down. Minshull Vernon station is gone, and with it the box from which Morris came down to look for the train which never arrived. Gone too with the station is a convenient name for this accident, which took place close to the deserted site.

Indeed the question of naming accidents looks like being a minor problem on the new-style railways. With wayside stations and signal boxes being steadily wiped off the map, what are we to do for a name? In this case the official title is: 'Between Winsford Station and Coppenhall Junction'; I have used what seems the most appropriate short title. There are other more important disabilities from which the modern railway system, cut off from its local environment, suffers, as we shall see.

The grim winter of 1962-63 had already set in in the North. It was freezing hard, with snow on the ground, though clear. The time was about 6 p.m. Frozen points at Crewe had caused a pile-up of trains waiting to enter the station from the north. Halted at No. 110 light, about 1½ miles south of Winsford, was the 4.45 p.m. from Liverpool to Birmingham, its eight coaches well filled with 300 Christmas travellers and hauled by one of the new blue 3300 h.p. electric locomotives. At the previous light, No. 114, not quite a mile to the rear, stood the up Mid-day Scot, with thirteen coaches likewise filled with 500 passengers and hauled by 2200 h.p. English Electric diesel No. 326.

The Birmingham train's fireman (they were still using the old term for the diesel or electric driver's mate) had tried to phone Coppenhall box, but without success. Then the driver, Hedgcock, tried, with no better result. No wonder; all the up line telephones had been put out of order by a trifling fault arising from a previous call; to an outsider it seems a very vulnerable system. Here again we encounter the venerable Rule 55 concerning a train standing at a signal, which we first learned about at Hawes Junction fifty-two years before. It is still in operation, but modified to suit present-day conditions. With a lineside telephone at each light the fireman is spared a journey to the box; indeed the nearest one may be a long way away. But suppose the telephone is out of action? In that case, says the current Rule, a driver may proceed to the next stop signal 'if he can see or ascertain that the line is clear'. Then someone at headquarters had a bright idea: why not use the phone on the other line? It will lead to the wrong box, of course, but the signalman there can pass on the message to the man in the right box. So Hedgcock's fireman went to the nearest down telephone and called up Winsford. He was told to wait until the signal cleared.

The fireman and driver of the Mid-day Scot were having the same trouble at light 114. First one tried, then the other, then both tried on the slow line telephone. These various attempts had taken up a good six minutes when the driver lost patience. Bother the telephones. Bother the regulations. Never mind about the instruction to use the down line phone, which looked a long way off anyway (it was—nearly 500 yards). Never mind that he could neither see nor had tried to ascertain if the line was clear to the next signal. The red glow of No. 110 beckoned in the distance. 'We have wasted enough time in the section', said the driver to his mate. 'The road looks clear ahead to signal No. 110, and we will make for there'. With that he set off.

Sheer stupidity, I have called his action, and even that seems too mild a word. It was the nearest thing to wilful negligence that we come across anywhere in this book. Yet perhaps we should make allowance for the attitude of a driver nurtured in steam, who could not readily adapt himself to the new motive units. This driver was sixty-three and had driven steam engines for twenty-five years. Though he had been on diesels for the past twelve months we have to infer that he was not reconciled to them yet, and it seems to me that resentment may have had something to do with his impatience. I will not name him, but he was a Scotsman, from the Motive Power Depot (new fancy name for engine shed) at Polmadie, Glasgow. Now the Scots have shown a peculiar genius for steam, whether on railways or in ships; Scottish engine drivers as a body were probably the best in Britain. When the Midland compounds, for example, were made a standard L.M.S. design and the North Western drivers could make nothing of them, the Scottish men got better work out of them even than the drivers on the parent line. A driver who has taken pride in his craft skill—in 'wrestling with them', as a driver once put it to me—will not take kindly to a machine which operates at the turn of a handle. (Another sort of driver, of course, welcomes it as less hard work.) We surely discern the abiding steam mentality in the words: 'We have wasted enough time in the section'. A diesel or electric driver needs to worry less about delays, since it is far easier for him to recoup them.

So much is conjecture; the next is fact. It is clear that the driver did not even consider the possibility of a train standing at the next light. Therein lay his stupidity, for apart from the remote chance of a signal failure, what can a red light mean except that there is a train in the section ahead? But with an amazingly un-Scottish lack of caution neither the driver nor the fireman kept any sort of proper lookout, nor apparently did they observe the speedometer. Here again I think that steam experience led them astray. The speedometer, a standard fitting in many Continental countries, never found favour in Britain; I believe that only the Great Western 'Kings' were fitted with it as an entire class. So British drivers have been accustomed to judge speed by the rail joints, the exhaust or the passing track. The diesel or electric driver, in his enclosed cab, has no aid from the locomotive, for the sound of the power unit does not necessarily vary with the speed of the train. If also as in this case the rails are welded the driver has no help from the rail joints either. None of this matters of course provided he keeps a watch on his speedometer, but our driver was not the sort of man to do that. Moreover these engines' speedometers are not marked below 10 m.p.h., which at a casual glance can be mistaken for 0, so that if the driver did look at his speedometer he probably misread it. That is the only possible excuse—a limp and partial excuse—for his action. Though he and his fireman claimed that they were travelling at no more than 5 m.p.h., and stuck to their story in the face of a time proof that it was impossible, in fact they were doing 20 to 25 m.p.h.

The Birmingham train's tail light could first have been seen 400 yards away. But the driver claimed that he was dazzled by the colour light, which just then had turned to yellow. He may have had some justification. The march of progress has passed the tail lamp by; its oil-lit flame is exactly the same as it was in the dawn of railways. A colour light, especially at yellow, throws an exceedingly powerful beam. But at over 100 yards away—still time to check speed—the light was obscured by the standing train, yet neither engineman noticed it. The driver had taken the yellow light, which of course was for the Birmingham train, as applying to himself. Only at twenty yards' distance, when the fireman shouted 'Stop', did he apply the brake. The Birmingham train had released its brakes, and Driver Hedgcock had put on power ready to start, when the diesel struck it.

The Birmingham train was pushed forward nearly fifty yards, and the two trains came to a stop a few yards apart. The coaches of both were fitted with buck-eye couplings, but even these are not always proof against such violent shocks. The coupling between the eighth and seventh coaches of the Birmingham train fractured, and the former telescoped half-way into the other. It was lucky that the Birmingham train had already released its brakes, or the casualties would certainly have been greater. As it was, eighteen passengers were killed, all in the last two coaches.

I spoke of the modern railway system's disabilities. Here we encounter a most unhappy one; summoning help to an accident that has taken place in the wilds. If Minshull Vernon station had still been there help would have been called for at once. As it was, Driver Hedgcock phoned Winsford box within three minutes of the accident. He could see that it was a bad one and told the signalman so, but hearing about an accident is not the same as having seen it. The seriousness did not register with the signalman, who did nothing about calling help for another twenty-five minutes, when he phoned the porter at Winsford station. The porter made an emergency call at once, but then there was further delay in locating the site. Meanwhile Ticket Collector Mulhearn from the Mid-day Scot had run across the fields to a farm, but the telephone there was out of order, and someone had to go on a motor bicycle to another farm, and after that more time was lost finding out exactly where the accident had occurred. So a whole hour elapsed before the first ambulances made their way across the frostbound fields. It transpired, too, that the signalmen, though each had a diagram of the signals connected with him, had no idea just where any of those signals might be. Surely someone, somewhere, thought the Inspecting Officer, ought to have a map on which the signals were marked.

The accident revealed yet another disability, which has been repeated since in a minor mishap outside Liverpool Street, concerned with overhead electrification. The rear coach of the Birmingham train had struck the wires as it was pushed forward, which put the whole section out of action. Five electric trains in the vicinity were immobilized, and steam and diesel locomotives had to be sent to fetch them in.

No. 326 was not much damaged. She was at work again to be the engine concerned in the Great Train Robbery a few months later. An unlucky engine indeed.

It would be kindest to regard Winsford No. 2 as an accident of transition, which for that reason is unlikely to recur. As drivers become used to the new forms of power, and a fresh generation grows up which does not have to try to unlearn so much of what it learned in steam, we can hope that accidents caused by drivers' errors will become a thing of the past, just as accidents caused by signalman's errors have become nearly impossible on the modernized lines. Can we prophesy that some future chronicler will be able to record Winsford No. 2 as the last great British railway accident?

INDEX